W9-AKV-974

—PEOPLE TO KNOW—

WILL ROGERS

Cowboy Philosopher

Mary Malone

ENSLOW PUBLISHERS, INC.

44 Fadem Road	P.O. Box 38
Box 699	Aldershot
Springfield, N.J. 07081	Hants GU12 6BP
U.S.A.	U.K.

Library of Congress Cataloging-in-Publication Data

Malone, Mary.
    Will Rogers: cowboy philosopher / Mary Malone.
       p. cm. — (People to know)
    Includes bibliographical references and index.
    Summary: Follows the private and public life of the humorist and social critic,
from his childhood in Oklahoma through his years as a cowboy to his rise to fame
as an entertainer.
    ISBN 0-89490-695-X
    1. Rogers, Will, 1879-1935—Juvenile literature. 2. Entertainers—United
States—Biography—Juvenile literature. 3. Humorists, American—Biography—
Juvenile literature. [1. Rogers, Will, 1879-1935. 2. Entertainers. 3. Humorists.
4. Cherokee Indians—Biography. 5. Indians of North America—Biography.]
I. Title. II. Series.
PN2287.R74M36   1996
792.7'028'092—dc20
[B]   95-32149
                                          CIP
                                          AC

Printed in the United States of America

10 9 8 7 6 5 4 3 2 1

Illustration Credits:
Courtesy of the California Department of Parks and Recreation, pp. 55, 73,
82, 84; Courtesy of the Will Rogers Memorial, Claremore, Oklahoma,
pp. 4, 11, 13, 20, 22, 29, 31, 37, 42, 45, 49, 57, 61, 68, 78, 91, 93, 97,
105, 112.

Cover Illustration:
Courtesy of the California Department of Parks and Recreation

Contents

Will Rogers as he appeared in the *Follies*.

"Will Rogers' remarks are not only humorous but illuminating."[1]

—President Woodrow Wilson

The *Follies*

Will Rogers, in the beginning of his career, was a vaudeville performer whose talents were his roping skills and his folksy monologues. When he was hired to perform in the *Ziegfeld Follies*, that was the big break he needed to secure his niche in show business. It was also the beginning of a friendship between the warm and friendly Oklahoma cowboy and the cold, distant theater impresario Florenz Ziegfeld. Will Rogers never managed to pronounce Ziegfeld's name properly, calling him Ziegfield and addressing him as "Boss." Ziegfeld in time stopped referring to Rogers as "that cowboy" and had to acknowledge the tremendous appeal of the "ropin' fool," as Rogers called himself.

Florenz Ziegfeld had opened his first *Follies* show in 1907 in the New Amsterdam Theater in New York City.

A Parisian-type revue, the *Follies* combined many of vaudeville's aspects, but in a more elegant way. Its central feature was the chorus of beautiful women in lavish costumes, amid spectacular scenery and effects. Acts by well-known singers, dancers, and comedians were inserted between the chorus numbers. With the addition of Will Rogers in 1915, the *Follies* had a new act—a cowboy who roped and joked.

Will Rogers had started in the *Frolic*, an offshoot of the *Follies*, because Ziegfeld's manager, Gene Buck, had seen him in vaudeville. Buck thought the cowboy's act would go over big in the informal atmosphere of the *Frolic*. Ziegfeld doubted that, but he agreed to give Rogers a chance to perform in the sophisticated midnight supper show. Will Rogers proved to be a big hit on the "Roof," as he called the *Frolic*, which was played on the roof of the New Amsterdam Theater. Sometime later, when the *Follies* seemed to be lagging in popularity, Ziegfeld himself asked Rogers to join it, in order to inject some light-hearted humor into the beautiful but somewhat dull extravaganza. Will Rogers and his act soon became the most popular part of the revue. For several years, he played in both shows, upstairs and down, being careful not to repeat in the *Frolic* the same jokes he told in the *Follies*. Based on what he read in the newspapers, his jokes touched on all aspects of life, but his prime targets were politicians, Congress, and big-name persons in the business and banking worlds. Although timely, his jokes or "gags," were never offensive and never off-color, and so did not require "laundering," as he said.[2]

However, one evening in the spring of 1916, when he learned, right before a performance, that President Woodrow Wilson and Mrs. Wilson were to be in the *Follies* audience, Rogers became very nervous. Although he was always a bit nervous before he started his act, he relaxed as soon as he was on. But this was different. In previous performances, he had made jokes related to the President's policies and to government bungling. Some jokes he planned to tell this evening could be inappropriate. He was about to face the biggest man in the country. "I am not kidding you when I tell you that I was scared to death," he said. "How was I to know but what the audience would rise up in mass . . . ? I had never heard . . . of a President being joked personally in a Public Theater."[3]

When the time came for his act, Rogers' friends backstage had to push him out to face the spotlights. Standing there, ducking his head, grinning sheepishly, he started off by saying, "I'm kinder nervous here tonight."[4] That was so obvious that the audience roared with laughter, the President included, as Rogers noticed.

He warmed up little by little, becoming reassured whenever he glanced at the presidential box to see the reaction there. The President and Mrs. Wilson seemed to be enjoying themselves thoroughly. One of the several jokes Rogers managed to tell was about the President being many notes behind in the exchange of diplomatic notes with Germany. (This was before the United States entered World War I.) Rogers was delighted when he saw the President laughing as heartily as everyone else in the theater.

When intermission arrived, the President went backstage and shook hands with everyone in the show. Rogers said it was the proudest night he ever had, one of "the happiest moments of my entire career on the stage."[5]

President Wilson attended several *Follies* shows in later years. Will Rogers was not only the popular featured player in those productions, he was on his way to becoming as big a celebrity as any of those he spoofed.

". . . there's nothing of which I am more proud than my Cherokee blood."[1]

—Will Rogers

Oklahoma

The Will Rogers story begins, not in Oklahoma where he was born, but in the Cherokee Nation of the state of Georgia. After being settled there for many years, the Cherokees, along with other Native American tribes, were forced from their homeland in 1838 by government decree during the term of President Andrew Jackson. The Cherokee people had to travel thousands of miles to land set aside for them beyond the Mississippi River. Their harrowing journey west has been called the "Trail of Tears" because of the hardships and the many deaths suffered on the way. In a shameful episode of American history, the Cherokee people's possessions in some of the states they had to leave—their land, cattle, horses, and houses—were taken over and distributed by lotteries to the white inhabitants of the district.

Of all the Native American peoples, the Cherokees were considered to be among the most intelligent and industrious. They were literate in English as well as their own language, and many were well educated. Some of Will Rogers' ancestors were among the white men who married Cherokee women and became part of the civilized Cherokee Nation in Georgia. But in 1835, foreseeing what was soon to happen, Will's grandfather, Robert Rogers, along with some others, packed up their families and left before the government-forced migration. They arrived in what would be established as Indian Territory, later to be part of the state of Oklahoma. Robert Rogers was enterprising and hard-working, and lost no time in claiming land, free to the Cherokee people (including those like himself, who were of mixed ancestry), and becoming a successful rancher. He married Sallie Vann, who was also part Cherokee, and in 1839, their son Clement Vann Rogers was born.

In his youth, Clem Rogers was strikingly like what his son, Will Rogers, would be—independent, restless, adventuresome. He left home at age seventeen, bought some livestock, and staked out his own ranch land near the Verdigris River in the Indian Territory. He built a log house and married Mary America Schrimsher.

Most of the Cherokees supported the Southern cause after the Civil War began in 1861. Their chief, Stand Watie, was a brigadier general in the Confederate Army,

Will Rogers' mother, Mary America Schrimsher Rogers.

and he attracted to that side many Cherokees. Clem Rogers was among them; he served under Stand Watie for four years. When Clem returned home, after Mary Rogers had gone for safety to her parents in Texas, he found that the Cherokee land had been overrun and ruined; cattle and horses were gone, dwellings destroyed. Clem Rogers spent the next several years working for a mill owner, driving a freight wagon to faraway settlements. When he had saved enough money, he bought some cattle and returned to the rich grazing land near the Verdigris River not far from his former place. As a member of the Cherokee Nation, he was allowed to claim as much land as he could occupy and improve. He brought Mary Rogers back home, and in a few years, he built a fine home for her and their children. This house, the Rogers homestead, was an outstanding structure for that time and place. It was two stories high, plastered and weatherproofed, painted white, with large rooms and open fireplaces, and equipped with the best furniture Clem Rogers could buy. The Rogers family owned the only piano for miles around.

In time, Clem became the prosperous owner of one of the largest ranches in the territory, located a few miles from tiny Oologah, a whistle-stop on the Missouri-Pacific Railroad. The nearest sizable town was Claremore, ten miles south.

Eight children were born to Clem and Mary Rogers. Three died in infancy, as was so common in those days,

The Rogers family homestead in Indian Territory, Oklahoma, was an outstanding structure for that time and place.

when there were no vaccines available to prevent childhood diseases. Five Rogers children, three daughters and two sons, survived. The youngest, and last, of the children was born on November 4, 1879, and he was named William Penn Adair Rogers. The boy would be called "Willie" by his family, and "Will" by his friends. In April 1883, when he was three, his older brother, Robert, died. This left Willie as the only son in the family. He was made much of—not only by his parents, but also by his three sisters, Sallie, Maude, and May, all of whom took good care of their baby brother.

Willie was given everything he wanted. "No boy in the Indian Territory had more than Uncle Clem's boy," Betty Rogers, Will's wife, wrote years later.[2] She wanted to disprove the popular notion that Will Rogers had been born poor. The Rogers family were the first to buy such new things as the first rubber-tired buggy in Oologah. They took railroad trips to the nearest cities, St. Louis and Kansas City, Missouri, and to big events like the 1893 Chicago World's Fair. When Willie was only five, he received his first pony. He was lifted into the saddle by his father and watched anxiously by his mother. "Clem," she called, "you're going to get my boy killed."[3] Willie himself, however, was agile as well as fearless when it came to handling animals. He had a special bond with the horses he owned and worked with throughout his life. "I was born bowlegged so I could sit on a horse," he said.[4]

Only a few years after getting his first pony, Willie took part in a roundup on the ranch. His father assigned a trusted cowboy to look after him. Another cowboy, an African-American man called Uncle Dan Walker, was the boy's first teacher in the art of throwing a rope. (In the Cherokee Nation, most adult males were called "Uncle.") Under Uncle Dan's guidance, lassoing became Willie's passion. He spent hours with the old cowboy, trying to learn all the tricks of the rope. As he grew older, he became adept, practicing constantly, always working to improve his skill. He would loop a rope around his saddle when riding his horse, so that it was handy if he saw something to lasso.

Willie was popular with his boyhood companions— white, black, and Cherokee. They all raced their horses, commonly referred to as "ponies," and roped calves at an early age. In those days and in that territory, roping was a popular sport. Another pastime with boys on the ranch was riding to the river, then leading the animals into the water and grabbing their tails as the horses swam to the other side.

Willie and his cousin Spi Trent were partners in fun, and they played practical jokes, sometimes on each other. Once Willie managed to pack a load of firecrackers in Spi's back pants pocket. When Spi sat down, the firecrackers went off, and he streaked out of the house, hollering as he ran. The whole household came out to watch the commotion, and Willie was soundly scolded. Spi promised to get even, but being three years younger than Willie, he had a hard time keeping up with his cousin. Their relationship remained firm, however, with Spi willing to join Willie in whatever mischief was planned.

If Willie did not become a lawyer or a banker, both occupations that his father favored, he would have the ranch to run, and he needed a lot of direction and training in the meantime. He could not be allowed to go his own way, because as Clem Rogers often said, "There's a lot of mule in Willie."[5] When school began, the fun stopped for Willie, and he was shipped off to get an education.

"I have regretted all my life that I did not at least take a chance on the fifth grade."[1]

—Will Rogers

School Days

From the time he was seven until he was eighteen, Will Rogers attended several schools. The first one was near the house of his oldest sister, Sallie, who had married Tom McSpadden. Will stayed at their house and rode his pony to school. At recess time, Will and the other boys had fun racing their ponies. That was the only thing Will liked about school. He hated the drills, and he hated being inside the schoolroom. When it became obvious that he was not learning, the principal notified his family, and Will was sent to a church school where his sister May was a pupil. Will and the headmaster's son were the only boys, and it was not long before Clem Rogers was told that Will was not doing well. It was suggested that he be removed.

About this time, tragedy struck the Rogers family again. Will's mother grew ill after caring for her daughters Maude and May, who had contracted typhoid fever. Although the girls recovered, their mother died. Will was only ten years old. He cried, even years later, whenever he talked about it, which was seldom. "My mother's name was Mary," he said once, "and if your mother's name was Mary and she was an old-fashioned woman, you don't have to say much for her. Everybody knows already."[2]

That fall, Will was sent to his third school, but he became even more indifferent to learning, and failed there too. Then his father settled upon Halsell College, a private boarding school. Will spent three years at Halsell, where he already knew many of the students from his neighborhood. As always, he was the class clown, popular with his classmates, if not with his teachers. He was good at reciting famous speeches, putting the emphasis on the wrong parts and making faces. His recitations entertained his listeners, who began to laugh even before he started to speak. Although he maintained later that he never got out of the fourth-grade reader, he did fairly well in history as well as elocution. He had a remarkable memory, and years later, he could remember the names of all his classmates at Halsell.

In the meantime, changes in the administration of the Indian Territory were to affect the lives of the ranchers. Most of them, like Clem Rogers, belonged to the Cherokee Nation by right of their Cherokee ancestors, although they were more white than Cherokee. Around 1890, Clem perceived that the government movement to open up the Cherokee Strip—a large part of northern Oklahoma—to incoming settlers was soon going to result in breaking up the ranches. He moved into Claremore and became a leading citizen there, working actively for the welfare of the Cherokees. When their lands were taken over, the Cherokees received partial compensation, but the size of their holdings was drastically cut. Clem Rogers' ranch was reduced to a fraction of its former size, and he began farming. Growing up, Will was reluctant to follow his father's wishes for him to run the ranch—what was left of it—after he finished his education. Farming was more distasteful than ranching, in Will's eyes, now that the old cowboy life on the ranch with its cattle drives and roundups was over.

After Halsell, Will was sent to Scarritt Collegiate Institute, a boarding school in Missouri. Again he was an indifferent student. As he grew older, his skill in roping, honed by constant practice, increased, and he never traveled anywhere without a lasso. To hide the rope from school authorities, he wrapped it around his waist, under his shirt or coat. Eventually it was discovered, and all the ropes in his possession were confiscated. He usually found makeshift lariats anyway. He roped everything that moved, even his classmates—especially the girls.[3]

Will Rogers' father, Clem Rogers, became a leading citizen in Claremore, Oklahoma.

One day, using an old rope that had been tied around a trunk, he tried to lasso the headmaster's mare and her foal, peacefully grazing in a meadow. The rope slipped and resulted in both horses bolting, the foal with the rope hanging from his neck. The excitement that this caused hastened Will's dismissal. The headmaster said that Will might not be able to get along without his lariat, but the school could get along without Will. He had acquired a reputation not only for his roping, but for practical jokes and classroom disruption. A girl he had asked to a party said her mother would not let her go out with a "wild Indian boy."[4]

Clem Rogers withdrew his son after one year at Scarritt. He hoped that the strict discipline of a military school would tame the boy, so Will was packed off again, in January 1897, this time to Kemper Institute in Boonville, Missouri. There were some things about Kemper that Will liked—the uniform, and drilling with a rifle. He participated in football and baseball. He still practiced with his lariat every chance he could get. Although he received demerits and his ropes were taken away when he was caught with them, Will never considered giving up his favorite pastime. He accumulated so many demerits that he had to spend hours marching around the school grounds to work them off.

Billy Johnston, a friend at Kemper, told Will about the big cattle ranches in Texas, where he came from.

Will Rogers (seated, right) poses with some of his friends at the Kemper Institute.

Before long, Will decided to go to Texas. He did not tell his father, but he wrote to his sisters asking to borrow money. They sent him enough to pay his railroad fare, and at eighteen, Will took off for Texas. "When he left Kemper, he was up to his neck in penalties," his cousin Spi said.[5]

Social Life

Will Rogers, as he said, "dragged" in at the Ewing ranch in Higgins, Texas, which Billy Johnston had mentioned, and was grateful to be accepted there.[2] Fortunately, W. P. Ewing knew Will's father and he wrote a letter to Clem Rogers telling him that Will was safe and sound. What should they do with him? Clem Rogers wrote back suggesting that Ewing get whatever work he could out of the young man. It was not a glowing recommendation, and Will was aware that he was a disappointment to his father. He was sorry about that, but he also was sure that he could never follow Clem's prescription for success in running the downgraded ranch. It contained "manual work" or "day labor," which Will maintained he wanted to avoid.[3] Working for several months on the Ewing ranch as a cowboy was not manual work as he saw it.

Roping, branding, and rounding up cattle was fun—dangerous fun, sometimes, such as walking on top of cattle cars when cows were being shipped by rail. As Spi Trent said, Will had a kind of surefootedness about him.[4]

When Will had enough money saved, he bought an old horse and left for Amarillo, Texas. He planned to sign up with Colonel Theodore Roosevelt's Rough Riders, a regiment of the United States Cavalry volunteers, that was about to depart for action in the Spanish-American War of 1898. He was turned down, however, because he was thought to be too young. He then joined an outfit driving a herd of cattle to Kansas. After that, he returned home to Oologah.

Clem Rogers hoped his son would settle down at that point, manage what was left of the old ranch, and live in the homestead. Clem restocked the ranch with cattle and allowed Spi to help Will. The house where Will had spent a happy childhood with his mother was now being run by a tenant farmer and his wife. The place was neglected and run down; even the food the farmer's wife cooked was not to Will's liking, so he and Spi moved out on the range into a log cabin they built themselves. Here the two young men managed to stay for several months. They ate navy beans three times a day, and any visitors were told to help themselves from an old iron kettle always full of Will's favorite food. One night, the two horses Will had tied to the house, frightened by a storm, shied away and pulled down the cabin. By this time the tenant farmer and his wife had moved away, and Will's sister May and her husband had taken over the ranch house. Will moved back in and found life there much more comfortable.

During this period, he seemed to have settled down somewhat. He owned cattle, he enjoyed taking part in the roping contests that were held in the area, and he became expert at roping both steers and calves. He had a little yellow horse called Comanche that his father had bought as a colt and had given to him. Will had broken and trained the horse himself, and on Comanche he was able to rope, tie, and throw a steer in record time. Comanche was speedy and smart; he seemed to sense what his rider wanted done, and together they worked in such harmony that Will refused all offers to buy him: "there is not enough money in that grandstand to buy old Comanche," he told one would-be buyer.[5]

Although to Will the roping and hog-tying of steers was sport, there was danger enough to keep a surefooted cowboy alert. At one roping contest, after he had roped and tied a large steer, the animal managed to get up and make straight for him. Leonard Trainer, an expert roper who was watching, called out "Fall flat, Will! Fall flat!"[6] Will reacted fast and dropped flat on his stomach. The steer jumped right over him and kept on going. Will was pale and shaken after his escape, but he never considered trying another line of work.

In 1899, when he was twenty, Will Rogers went to St. Louis, Missouri, for the annual fair and the roping and riding contests. There he met self-styled "Colonel" Zack Mulhall, who invited him to join a traveling troupe of musicians and cowboys. For a short time, Rogers was part of the Mulhall show which put on steer-roping contests after the band's performance. His experience with professional performers confirmed his dedication to roping and riding. That was the life for him, but he also learned that roping steers presented some problems.

After leaving the Mulhall troupe, Rogers and a friend went to the San Antonio, Texas, state fair, where the most famous steer-roping competitions were held. Celebrated cowboys who were roping champions vied for the big money prizes. One evening, after the day's events, Will struck up a conversation with Charles Tomkins, one of the cowboys. Tomkins recalled, years later, that Will Rogers was "small and a wiry-looking fellow, dark hair, and I knew at once that he had some Indian blood in him." When the cowboy learned that Rogers was planning to rope the next day, he thought to himself, as he said later, "you are pretty light to tackle those big wild steers."[7]

As it happened, Tomkins was right. In roping and tying a steer, Rogers finished eleventh in a field of nineteen—not good enough to rise to the top, or even make a living in roping steers. Both he and his beloved Comanche were too slight. Comanche, as he wrote later, "got . . . jerked down so many times they wanted me to tie the horse's feet instead of the steer's."[8] He began to think about his future.

Now a new interest entered Rogers' life—women. Will "cut a handsome figure," Jim Hopkins, a cowboy friend, said. "He was slim and dark, with high cheekbones and soulful eyes that bespoke his Cherokee heritage. . . . the greatest ladies man you ever saw."[9] Rogers liked dancing so much that he had a platform built at his ranch so he and his friends could stamp and reel in the popular dances of the time.

Rogers had several girlfriends who lived near Oologah, and he and cousin Spi went on double dates. One Sunday they attended church services with two young women they knew, and heard the minister urge the congregation to give as much as possible in order to pay off the church debt. "If you can't give anything," he added jocularly, "give a pleasant smile."[10] Rogers, with his love of practical jokes, seized on this chance to show off. When the basket came around, he gave nothing, but made sure the young women saw his wide grin. They were embarrassed and refused to go out with Will and Spi after that. However, the next day, Rogers sent the minister a check that covered the entire church debt. It was the minister who spread that news, not Will himself.

Kate Ellis, the local hotel keeper's daughter, was Rogers' girlfriend for a while. Through her, he met another young woman from the Ozark country who was

Will Rogers (second from left) and his cousin Spi Trent (second from right) often went on double dates.

visiting one of her sisters in Oologah. Her name was Betty Blake. She was the next to youngest of seven sisters and lived with her widowed mother in the town of Rogers, Arkansas. In Will Rogers' eyes, she outclassed all the other girls he knew. Betty Blake was not only pretty, with curly light brown hair and blue eyes, she was lively and friendly, and she played the piano. Kate Ellis had invited her for dinner along with Rogers because he had brought all the new songs from Kansas City. Kate was sure he would sing for them after dinner. Betty Blake noted that he was too shy at first, but after a while he thawed out and began to sing in a high tenor voice, accompanying himself on his banjo. The songs, including the most popular of the time—"Hello, My Baby, Hello, My Honey, Hello, My Ragtime Gal" and "I Wonder Who's Kissing Her Now"—were a big hit. Will gave Betty the music for the songs, and she promised to learn to play them. Before she left for home, they enjoyed musical evenings when he sang and she played the piano. While she was in Oologah, she participated in all the good times of that era—dances, picnics, hay rides, and Sunday strolls.

Will Rogers did not forget Betty Blake. Shortly after she reached home, she received her first letter from him. He addressed her as "My Dear Friend" and signed it as her "True Friend and Injun Cowboy, W P Rogers."[11] Betty replied, discreetly, after some time elapsed. Rogers' next letter was a bit more forward. It was "My Dear

30

Will Rogers (far right) and Betty Blake (in front, with black glove) enjoyed socializing with friends.

Betty" and he was—if she did not answer—"a broken hearted Cherokee Cowboy."[12] Will wrote that he knew she was meeting smooth young men in Arkansas, quite a contrast to him, an ignorant Cherokee cowboy, but none of them could think more of her than he did. Betty replied with less fervor than he hoped for. The two did not see each other for several months.

They met again by accident at an Arkansas fair, but Will felt that Betty's companions were teasing her about him, a rough, uncivilized cowboy, as he called himself. At a dance he avoided her, and Betty was surprised and hurt.[13] That was the last time they would meet for the next few years.

Will Rogers was getting restless again, ready to pull up stakes and leave home for new sights and experiences. To his father's chagrin, he had made it clear that managing a small herd of cattle in fenced pastures was not his idea of happiness. The old days of the Indian Territory were gone forever. Will decided he would go to Argentina. Although that sounded "outlandish," it was not unusual at the time.[14] After the Indian Territory was divided into allotments and farms, the thought of the huge ranches in South America attracted many young men in the territory. Few, however, had the means to travel there. His father tried to dissuade him, but Will was stubborn. He would go to Argentina. His only concession to his father was to take out a life insurance policy and agree to pay the premiums regularly while he was away. That, he declared, showed he was responsible. Clem Rogers then generously paid Will $3,000 for the cattle he had given his son when he was running the ranch. Will sold all his horses but Comanche, whom he entrusted to his father, with strict instructions about the horse's care. Then Will bade farewell to Oologah.

". . . I christened myself 'The Cherokee Kid'. . . ."[1]

—Will Rogers

The Cherokee Kid

Early in 1902, when he was twenty-two, Will Rogers "hit the trail" for Argentina. He was accompanied by a friend, Dick Parris, who was willing to go along because Rogers was paying the way. Both young men looked forward to adventure, and maybe to making a fortune.

They assumed that the logical place to get a ship going south was the port of New Orleans, but when they arrived there, they were told that the only way to South America led from New York City. So they went to New York, where they learned that if they really wanted to continue, they would have to go to England to get a ship for Argentina. Rogers was determined not to return to Oologah. He said they would carry on and go to England; Parris was still willing. On the ship to England, Rogers was seasick all the way; but he recovered rapidly when he and his friend, back on land, took in the sights of London before shipping off to Argentina. Then, for twenty-three days on the South Atlantic Ocean, Rogers was seasick again. He never got over seasickness, although in later years he felt somewhat better when he could afford to travel on ships that did not behave like a "bucking horse."[2]

The pair of travelers arrived at their destination and, not speaking Spanish, had to use sign language to get to the pampas—the prairies of Argentina. There Rogers learned, to his surprise, that the Argentine cowboys, called gauchos, could rope a steer "faster than I could hit him with a rock."[3] Rogers gave up the idea of trying to match such skill. He and Parris then spent five months knocking around the country, doing odd jobs for not much pay. Their money was rapidly disappearing, and Parris was too homesick to continue their trek. Rogers had to use almost the last of his money to pay for his friend's passage back to the United States. When Parris left, he carried home gifts of Brazilian lace from Rogers to his sisters.

When his funds were completely gone, Rogers had to sleep in a park. In order to get out of Argentina, he was willing to take any job he could get, on any outgoing ship. He took one "chaperoning" as he put it, a herd of mules on a steamer to South Africa.[4] That took thirty-one days of seasickness along with tending the sheep and cows that were also on board with the mules.

Finally landing in Durban, South Africa, in October 1902, he got a job with a horse trainer, taking care of and showing horses to prospective buyers. When he came upon a traveling American show called Texas Jack's Wild West Circus, he asked Texas Jack for a job. After he demonstrated his roping skill, he was hired. For almost a year he stayed with Texas Jack, traveling all over South Africa. He took a shot at almost every job in the circus. He was a clown, rope thrower, horse trainer, and part of the hard-riding, war-whooping Wild West finale of the circus performance. Will Rogers was called the "Cherokee Kid," and his war whoops were so terrifying to audiences that he was asked to stop them. However, he learned a great deal about show business from Texas Jack, especially the art of roping while riding a horse, instead of twirling a lasso while standing on the ground.

Rogers wrote regularly to his father, and he also managed to send enough money to keep up the payments on his life insurance policy. Sometimes he had a hard time getting the money together. He never made more than the equivalent of $25 a week while working in the circus. In one letter, he instructed his father to send "100 feet of the best kind of hard twist rope. . . . Please send this at once."[5] He always signed his letters "your loving son, Willie."[6] In another letter, he told his father that he was making out fine. "I still keep sober, and don't gamble, and [Texas] Jack thinks a lot of me. I'm going to learn things while I'm with him that will

Will Rogers (far right) was called the Cherokee Kid in Texas Jack's Wild West Circus. Texas Jack (far left) taught Rogers a great deal about show business.

enable me to make my living in the world without making it by day labor."[7] Before he left South Africa, Rogers wrote to his father that he would be back in Indian Territory in about three months. It was over a year, however, before he made it home. He had first to go by way of Australia and New Zealand in order to make enough money for his return passage. When he arrived in Australia after thirty days of seasickness, he had a letter of recommendation from Texas Jack. That won him a job with the Wirth Brothers Circus, which traveled around Australia and New Zealand. He became a good friend of the Wirth family. He did roping as well as daring tricks on his horse. When he performed as the Mexican Rope Artist, he wore an outfit Mrs. George Wirth made for him—a bright, tight red velvet suit trimmed with gold braid.

In off-hours, Rogers took part in racing meets in order to earn more money. One day, the governor-general of Australia was present among the spectators when the "Cherokee Kid" did a trick bending backward over the horse's rump to pick up three handkerchiefs from the ground. The governor-general was impressed and asked to see the trick again. To the messenger sent with the request, Rogers said "he would do it again for thirty pounds" (equal to $150).[8] That was refused by the official, but people in the crowd collected $150, and Rogers performed his handkerchief trick again.

Eventually he had enough money to book a

third-class passage from New Zealand to San Francisco. From there, he rode on freight trains until he reached Oologah. He wrote later that when he first left the United States he "started out first class, dropped to second class, and came home third class. But when I was companion to those cows . . . it might be called no class at all."[9] He had been away for more than two years. When he finally arrived in Oologah in April 1904, the wanderer was penniless, but he had a lot of stories to tell about his adventures. Maybe his father did not appreciate the stories, but Clem Rogers did gather all the family and relatives together for a big celebration of his son's return home.

"I was the first one ever to rope a horse on the stage." [1]

—Will Rogers

Riding and Roping

Clem Rogers welcomed his son home, and listened as the returned traveler talked glowingly about his exciting show business performances. In Clem's eyes, however, being a circus cowboy was not a career to count on. And it seemed that the Rogers' only son was committed to that. Soon after he returned home, he heard from his old friend, Colonel Zack Mulhall, who wanted him to join a troupe of riders and ropers in the Wild West show he was putting on at the 1904 St. Louis World's Fair. Will Rogers accepted the offer and joined the Mulhall family. They treated him like a son, and he and Lucille, one of the Mulhall daughters, became quite friendly. She was an accomplished cowhand who could rope and tie a steer as quickly as a man. Rogers thought she was also very pretty.

Mrs. Zack Mulhall owned a beautiful little bay horse with a black mane and tail. When she saw how much Rogers admired him, she offered to sell him for $100, which was a bargain. He still had Comanche, his roping horse, but the new one would be ideal for the stage work he was planning. He bought the horse from Mrs. Mulhall with the first $100 he could save, and named him Teddy, after President Theodore Roosevelt. He began training Teddy, and together they formed a partnership that lasted several years.

While Rogers was performing at the fair, Betty Blake happened to be in St. Louis visiting one of her sisters. She was walking with her sister and a young woman friend through the Oklahoma state exhibit building when they heard someone say that Will Rogers was performing in the Wild West show. They bought tickets to see the show, and Betty Blake sent a note to her former "beau." A reply came quickly—an invitation to supper after the show. When Rogers met the young women, he was wearing the Mexican rope artist suit Mrs. Wirth had made for him in Australia. He was trying to look his best in order to impress Betty. However, she was not impressed, as he could see from her expression. He realized that she was embarrassed by his flamboyant outfit.[2] He never wore that suit again.

Betty Blake returned home to Arkansas, and Will Rogers continued to travel with the Mulhalls. He wrote to her often. He said in one letter that he knew

Will Rogers with his horse, Comanche. He later bought a second horse, named Teddy, from Mrs. Zack Mulhall.

"a cowboy dident (sic) come up to your Ideal," but as for himself, "I could just love a girl about your caliber."[3] If she was not yet married, he wanted to file his application. She did not reply as warmly as he would have liked, so in one of his next letters, he told her that her last letter to him "was on the chilly side;" he had "to take to my overcoat to read it. . . ."[4]

Rogers continued his riding and roping act with the Mulhalls and began to hope that maybe someday he could break into vaudeville, then in its heyday as the most popular entertainment wherever there was a theater. He might be more respectable in Betty Blake's eyes in vaudeville than in a circus. Texas Jack had told Rogers that a roping act with a pony could be a stage hit. Rogers believed that such an act would be new and original in vaudeville. Now that he had Teddy, he felt ready to try it.

When the Mulhall troupe was engaged to go to New York City to put on a riding and roping exhibition in Madison Square Garden, Rogers signed on as one of the featured ropers. Besides getting paid for what he loved to do, he was eager to see New York again. While he was with the Mulhalls he had made friends, among them Tom Mix, who would later become a famous cowboy movie star.

It was at Madison Square Garden that Rogers got the break that would start his big career in show business. Lucille Mulhall was roping on the tanbark—the circus ring—when an eight-hundred-pound steer ran unexpectedly into the ring and jumped into the stands. Pandemonium ensued. The spectators rushed to get out of the way and Colonel Mulhall, standing below, bellowed an order to Lucille, in effect, to "Get that baby down!" Rogers, who had been roping calves in the ring, ran after the steer, which was by this time making for the stairs to the balcony. With a great display of his roping skill, Rogers hurled his lasso several feet in the air and caught the animal's horns. Keeping his distance, he made the steer swerve down the steps, and when the huge animal jumped back into the ring, it was roped by other cowboys and led away.

The newspapers featured the story, praising the "Indian Cowpuncher," Will Rogers, for his skill and daring and his quick action in preventing harm. The former Cherokee Kid was described in print as "the finest ropeman in the world,"[5] a cowboy who could use two lassos at once. This was heady stuff, and although Rogers himself would not claim that it was all true, he did send clippings from the newspapers back home to Claremore. The publicity also brought him and a roping friend, J. H. Minnick, an invitation from the White House to perform some of their tricks for President Theodore Roosevelt's children.

Rogers still had no vaudeville work, so he began to think about forming his own company, and made an impulsive decision to go to Europe with it. Cowboys

Will Rogers was friends with Lucille Mulhall. Like Rogers, Mulhall was an accomplished cowhand who could rope and tie a steer quickly.

were a novelty over there, and he would have no competition. That would satisfy his recurring wanderlust too, and his desire to see new places, to meet people, and to see how the rest of the world lived. Besides himself and his "pony" Teddy, he planned to take a partner, Buck McKee, and several additional cowboys and horses. Shipping all his paraphernalia took a lot of arranging.

After reaching Europe, Rogers performed in England and Germany. He was quite successful in an act that was considered pure Americana. In Germany he met the kaiser (on horseback in the park), and in England he met the prince of Wales at a polo exhibition. Rogers also learned that putting on his own show was not only hard to manage, but costly. He returned home more determined than ever to get into vaudeville, with Buck, Teddy, a couple of extra horses, and himself.

While abroad, he continued to send letters and small gifts to Betty Blake. In his letters he mentioned girlfriends, probably to try to make her jealous. She wrote back that she was seeing Tom Harvey, a young lawyer in Monte Ne, Arkansas, near her hometown.

When Rogers returned home to visit his father and sisters, he met Betty Blake again. This time he brought up the subject of marriage, but she gave him no encouragement. She made it clear—so it seemed—that traipsing all over the country, even the world, with a roving cowboy was not her idea of married life. If he were willing to settle down on his ranch in Oklahoma, she might be more willing, but he was not going to settle—yet—for that kind of life. He returned to New York, and he and Betty Blake still wrote to each other.

Rogers began to hang around the offices of the booking agents who could recommend would-be actors to different vaudeville houses. One of Will Rogers' biographers relates what happened then to a classic show business joke, often repeated in plays and movies. "Put this nut and his pony on at one of your supper shows," an agent said to a vaudeville producer, "and just get rid of them."[6] Keith's Union Square Theater accepted the advice, and Rogers was placed on the bill as a temporary "extra act." In his first trial performance with Teddy and Buck McKee, whom he roped in various ways, he pleased the audience. From the time he came on riding Teddy, who had felt boots on his hoofs to keep from sliding, Rogers gave the people at the show something different. They saw a selection from his amazing variety of fifty-three roping tricks, from small loops to big ones. Figure eights, the one called the Crinoline, which had impressed even Texas Jack, and the Umbrella, were done onstage, sometimes swishing over the heads of the audience to capture someone standing in the rear.

The New York Times called Rogers' act a "sensation," and his specialty "out of the ordinary." One of his best tricks was throwing two ropes at once, catching a running horse (Teddy) and rider (Buck McKee) separately. At baseball games, which he often attended, he would rope an entire team with his famous Crinoline.

Rogers' ropes were his stock-in-trade, and he took good care of them. Tom Mix, who shared a hotel room with him when they were together on a vaudeville circuit, said, "Every time I came in I stumbled over his ropes on the floor. Sometimes, when I got up at night, I would step on one and think I'd landed on a snake."[7]

Rogers was kept on at the Union Square Theater from week to week until the whole summer passed. His biggest problem was getting Teddy on the elevator to the roof of the theater, where the late supper show was performed.

After his initial success, he was sent to other vaudeville houses in New York and sometimes out of town. Eventually, he was booked at the Hammerstein's Theater in New York, where he was paid $140 a week, a big enough increase to convince him he was on the right track. For the next few years, he performed at Hammerstein's as well as taking engagements at theaters on the Orpheum vaudeville circuit. At first, his act was all action, no talk. The other performers at Hammerstein's would often watch from the wings as he performed.

One day, one of the actors told him that he ought to announce his tricks to the audience before he did them. Rogers agreed to try that, talking without any rehearsed speech. The first time, in his slow Oklahoma drawl, he

Will Rogers performed roping tricks all over—including baseball games. Here, he is on his horse Teddy, performing his famous Crinoline.

told the audience he was going to do a certain trick, and added, "I don't have any idea I'll get it, but here goes."[8] The audience laughed at that, but Rogers, still somewhat shy, was embarrassed.[9] He had not thought he said anything funny. He left the stage and told the manager he was going to quit. All of the performers backstage tried to convince him that the people were not laughing at him but with him, that they liked what he said.

Rogers was finally persuaded, and later admitted that deciding to talk as he roped was one of the luckiest things he ever did. He even started to "pull a gag," as he said, by deliberately getting tangled up in his rope and saying "swinging a rope is all right when your neck ain't in it."[10] From then on, he talked to his audience, in his own natural, folksy way, and his act became more popular than ever. His salary increased, although it varied from city to city. When he performed in Brooklyn, he reached the top—$250 a week—and his name was placed over the other vaudeville acts on the theater marquee. His father, who was informed of this, was beginning to take pride in his son's achievements, especially when people from Claremore saw the act and reported back to Clem about its success. Rogers himself liked what one of his father's cronies said after seeing the performance in New York. Asked by those at home what Willie was doing, the crony said, "Oh, just acting the fool like he used to do around here."[11]

However, Clem Rogers still could not understand

how anyone could make so much money in his son's line of work. "Two hundred and fifty dollars a week!," he exclaimed. "Looks like something is wrong somewhere."[12] But when he took his daughters Sallie and May to Washington, D.C., he attended every one of his son's headline performances at the theater. He even began counting the house to see how many people were in attendance. He told his daughters when they got back to their hotel one evening, "I tell you, girls, that manager sure is making a lot of money off Willie."[13]

Onstage

One day in November 1908, soon after his twenty-ninth birthday, Will Rogers made an unannounced visit to Betty Blake's home in Arkansas. He told her that they were going to be married—immediately. Betty, taken by surprise, or merely willing to be swept off her feet by something she had secretly hoped for, assented. Will was so happy he wrote GETTING MARRIED in the November 23 space in his engagement book, which he usually used solely for the dates of his vaudeville bookings.

Betty Blake made one condition. After his present tour was over, in the coming spring, they would return to Oklahoma and live on the ranch. She thought this would be a more stable kind of life than traveling all over the country. As soon as he had started making a good income, Rogers had restocked the old ranch with cattle and sheep, and hired his nephew, Herb McSpadden, his sister Sallie's son, to run it. He accepted Betty's condition.

The families of both bride and groom were present at the wedding ceremony in the Blakes' home on the day before Thanksgiving. Afterward, the newlyweds took the train to New York City. Rogers was scheduled to perform in nearby Newark, New Jersey, for the next two weeks. They had time for sightseeing every day between the matinee and evening shows. Will wanted to show Betty all the attractions of the big city. She enjoyed it all—going to plays, eating in restaurants, riding horseback in Central Park. The first musical comedy she ever saw was *The Red Mill,* starring Fred Stone, one of Rogers' best friends, whom he had met on the vaudeville circuit.

Betty loved the opera, and they went to several performances. Her husband did not share that enjoyment. He declared, "I hate to say it, but I enjoyed Grant's Tomb more cause I stayed outside while my wife went in."[2] To her surprise, Betty found that she was enjoying an easy life without home responsibilities. Rogers' schedule allowed them to spend a great deal of time together. "Come on, Blake, let's get going," he would say, and off they went.[3] He never seemed to rehearse any of his acts beforehand. He arrived at the theater with just a few minutes to spare before he took the stage.

Betty Rogers sat up front at every performance, giving approval as well as advice. One evening, the manager of the theater where Rogers was booked spoke to her about the act. He said that Will Rogers was so immensely popular himself that he could go it alone, without all the excess baggage of his act—the horses, the partners. Rogers, he believed, could hold the audience just by talking and joking as he twirled his ropes. Betty realized that she had been thinking along those lines, too, so she mentioned it to her husband. He agreed to try just being himself in an all-talk show. When he saw that audiences were attentive, he became more confident. He told jokes about the other actors in the show. He kidded them as well as people in the audience that he recognized.

One time he got into trouble and had to apologize. An act called The Cherry Sisters was on the same bill with him in one vaudeville theater. Rogers said that act must have been named before lemons were discovered.[4] After that mistake, he decided to do something Betty Rogers suggested—making jokes, or "gags," as he said, about what he read in the newspapers. That took him into politics, government, and world affairs. He began reading all the newspapers he could to keep up with happenings. "Well, all I know is just what I read in the papers,"[5] he said, often. It became his trademark phrase.

54

During his act, Will Rogers often made jokes about what he read in the newspapers.

In the daily newspapers, he found enough of the comical and the ridiculous to keep him well supplied with material for jokes.

Rogers made his comments while doing his rope tricks. Sometimes he would miss a throw on purpose, and then remark, "I've only got jokes enough for one miss." [6] When his trick was to jump inside a spinning loop, and he missed, he would gather the rope to make another try and say, "Well, got all my feet through but one."[7] Arriving onstage with a big wad of gum in his mouth, he would remove it if he missed a trick, parking it somewhere obvious; after he did the trick right, he retrieved the gum. He varied his routines. One day he missed a couple of times, then walked over to the sign with his name in big letters, and taking out his gum, put it over the W in Will Rogers. Such actions always brought a laugh from the audience.

Rogers' chief regret about performing alone was having to part with his horse Teddy and his loyal partner, Buck McKee. Buck was a cowboy as well as a former Oklahoma sheriff, and he had no trouble getting other jobs. Teddy was shipped back to the Rogers ranch in Oklahoma, where he lived in peaceful retirement.

In 1911, Will and Betty Rogers had their first child, a boy named William Vann Rogers. Called Bill as a youngster, he was referred to as Will Rogers, Jr., in later life. Clem Rogers lived just long enough to hear about

Will Rogers' roping tricks might include all the band members at the theater, as in this 1908 photo.

his new grandson, and to send the baby a pair of beaded moccasins. He died shortly afterward while on a visit to the home of his daughter Sallie. In tribute to him, because he had been a leading citizen in what was Indian Territory, and then in Oklahoma, Clem Rogers' home district was renamed Rogers County.

"If I can just stay natural I will be a hit."[1]

—Will Rogers

Star Performer
in the *Follies*

As a result of his success in vaudeville, Will Rogers was offered a part in the Broadway musical comedy *The Wall Street Girl.* He was to do a "specialty act," which really meant playing himself. His friend Fred Stone had encouraged him to take this opportunity to break into musical comedy. Fred was a big star in musical plays, being talented in both singing and dancing. The Stone and Rogers families maintained a close relationship, especially after Will and Betty Rogers, with their young son, moved into a rented house in Amityville, New York, just across the road from the Stones.

It was said of Will Rogers that although he did not jump at opportunities, he was always open to them if they were offered. He took the part in *The Wall Street Girl,* received good reviews, and went on tour with the play after it closed on Broadway; then he returned to vaudeville. While he was touring, Betty went with young Bill back to Arkansas, to her mother's home. In April 1913, the second Rogers child, a girl, was born. She was named Mary Amelia Rogers, after both grandmothers. With her sister Theda Blake helping to care for the children, Betty stayed in Arkansas for the next year. Will Rogers was away from home most of the time, trying to get ahead in the legitimate, nonvaudeville theater. He had a growing family and needed more income. Playing "special" parts (created just for him) in some musical comedies, he was affected when they all folded a short time after opening. He considered giving up on Broadway and returning for good to the vaudeville circuit, but Fred Stone advised him to stay on in New York. He would be available when an opportunity arose, not tramping around the country in vaudeville. Rogers took that advice, and as it turned out, he was ready when the best offer yet was extended to him, one that advanced his career and made him famous. By this time, the family was back in Amityville, where James Blake Rogers was born in July 1915.

Will Rogers took his first airplane ride in 1915. It was really a seaplane, anchored off Atlantic City, New Jersey, that provided his first trip aloft. He and Betty Rogers had gone there to watch some stunt fliers, and he decided to go up in the plane, anchored a short distance from shore. Betty stayed on land and watched as he was

Will and Betty Rogers' family grew in 1915, when James Blake Rogers was born. Shown here are Betty Rogers, and children Mary, Bill, and Jimmy.

taken out over the ocean for a short ride. It was not an especially impressive trip, but later Will Rogers would become one of the country's most ardent aviation boosters.

Also in 1915, Rogers bought the "pony" that he called "the greatest ever." He had an unfailing eye for good horses, a quality he inherited from his father. While in Connecticut one day, he saw a small coal-black horse that he liked, and he bought it immediately. Perfect in almost every respect, but as he said, "just the least bit lazy," the newest "pony" was named Dopey.[2] Dopey became the family pet, loved by the children, allowed inside the house. Each of the younger children was placed on Dopey for a first ride at the age of two, a birthday event. That little horse "helped raise our children," Rogers said, "during his lifetime, he never did a wrong thing. . . ."[3] Dopey took his place in Rogers' affection beside the special Comanche and Teddy. They all shared his life, onstage and off.

Rogers' big break, in the summer of 1915, was his engagement to play in Ziegfeld's *Midnight Frolic*, the late supper show for "folks with lots of money and plenty of insomnia."[4] When he proved to be a hit, Ziegfeld asked him to join the *Follies*, a bigger production that played in the same theater. Beautiful but a little dull, the *Follies* attraction improved when "the ropin' fool,"[5] as Rogers would call himself in one of his movies, was added to the cast. He became so popular over the next few years as the star of the show, that he was able to name his own salary. He stayed in the *Frolic*, too, for as long as it continued. He was modest about his great success in the *Follies*. He maintained that his act with the lasso was just put into the *Follies* to fill time. For several years, he went on tour with the *Follies* every fall after the New York season was over.

When the United States entered World War I in 1917, Will Rogers, at age thirty-eight, with a wife and three children, was exempt from the draft. He tried to make up for not serving actively in the war by pledging 10 percent of his salary to the Red Cross, and by participating in various fund-raising benefits for the soldiers. He even had his three children with him playing a benefit at the Polo Grounds in New York. One biographer, Donald Day, wrote that people there remembered "the amazement the little tykes created when they came galloping out, all mounted on their own ponies." Even Jimmy, called by his father the "Youngest cowboy in the world" at age two, was one of the riders.[6]

Rogers and his "kidding" continued at the *Follies*. People came just to see him and be kidded by him. He would single out celebrities in the crowd, make them stand up and be introduced, sometimes to other celebrities present. He did not do this unless he knew the person could "take a joke as it was meant," he said.[7] The popular novelist John O'Hara commented, "A big shot, a major industrial type, was not a confirmed tycoon until he had been kidded by Will Rogers."[8]

When Rogers left the *Follies* for Hollywood, he told his boss he would return whenever Ziegfeld wanted him. At his departure, Ziegfeld gave him a gold watch engraved "To Will Rogers, in appreciation of a real fellow, whose word is his bond."[9]

—Will Rogers

The California Life

Even before he left New York for Hollywood, Will Rogers had made his debut in movies. That happened in 1918 through his friendship with Fred Stone. Stone was the brother-in-law of the writer, Rex Beach. Samuel Goldwyn, one of the earliest movie producers, had bought one of Beach's novels, *Laughing Bill Hyde*, and was looking for an actor to play the lead in the movie version. At that time, the Stone family was on the West Coast, where Fred was making a movie, and the Rogers family was renting the Stones' house in Amityville, Long Island. Rex Beach's wife visited Betty and Will Rogers there and told them she suggested Rogers to Samuel Goldwyn as the ideal person to play Bill Hyde. Soon Goldwyn came to see him, and persuaded him to take the role in the movie, which Goldwyn promised would be filmed in a Fort Lee, New Jersey, studio so Rogers would not have to leave the *Follies*. As in many of his roles in other pictures later, Rogers played himself—informal, friendly, homespun. He never attempted anything but character roles that were markedly Will Rogers characters. The movie *Laughing Bill Hyde* was a critical success.[2]

Goldwyn then offered Rogers a contract to make pictures in Hollywood. He would be paid double what Ziegfeld was paying him for his appearances in the *Follies*. The money was welcome because by then there was a fourth Rogers child—Fred Stone Rogers, nicknamed Freddie, born in 1918. The prospect of moving to California and establishing a home there was just as attractive to Will and Betty as the money he would make in the movies. They had not purchased a home in the New York-area because they had some idea of eventually settling elsewhere, maybe in Oklahoma. So in 1919, Rogers left for California to look for a suitable house for his family. He found a satisfactory one in Los Angeles, then he sent for Betty and the children. When they arrived on the train, he met them in the big Overland touring car he had purchased in anticipation of his larger salary.

Rogers was on location much of the time. While at work one day, he was called home because the baby, Freddie, was very ill. All of the children had come down with diphtheria, a disease for which inoculations were not widely available at that time. The older children recovered, while Freddie grew worse. Rogers rode all night in order to locate the antitoxin that might save Freddie's life. He was too late, and little Freddie, only twenty months old, died.

Rogers could never bear to speak of his youngest son, just as he could not speak of his mother without tears. After the tragedy of Freddie's death, Will and Betty wanted to move away from the house where they had lived for such a short unhappy time. They found another place in Beverly Hills. On its several acres, there were stables for the horses, a riding ring for the children, and a polo field. This would be the family's home for nearly ten years.

Will Rogers made many silent films while he was under contract to Goldwyn. Besides acting in them, he often wrote the subtitles necessary to explain the dialogue. His acting was praised by critics for its naturalness, as contrasted with the more dashing style of actors like Douglas Fairbanks and William S. Hart. His contract with Goldwyn expired in 1921, at a time when the studios, including Goldwyn's, were in an unsettled state, cutting down the number of productions because many actors had started forming their own companies. Will Rogers decided that he, too, would go it alone. He started his company with the help of his wife and a hired director, and planned to produce, write, and act in his own films. To acquire enough money for his

The Rogers' ranch had a large riding ring for the children.

undertaking, he cashed in all of his assets, even mortgaging his house. He made three films in all. *One Day in 365* featured Betty Rogers and the children. It was a comic version of a hectic day in the life of the Rogers family. In another, *The Ropin' Fool*, he showed off his roping skills. The third, *Fruits of Faith*, featured the Rogers' son Jimmy. Delightful as the films were, however, they were not a financial success. Rogers turned them over to Pathé Films for possible distribution. He had lost thousands of dollars on his undertaking, and now he had to make money quickly to support his family and keep their home. Besides, he had started buying real estate on borrowed money and had to make high interest payments. He asked Ziegfeld to take him back in the *Follies*, and Ziegfeld agreed.

Rogers went alone to New York and while waiting for the *Follies* to open, he signed on for three weeks of vaudeville at the Schubert Theater. His fee for that was $8,000, said to be the highest salary ever paid in vaudeville. The many silent films he made in Hollywood had established him as a celebrity. When he opened again in the *Follies*, his name was in letters and lights as big as the show's name, but that did not prevent him from tackling other activities.

He started making speeches in a rather limited way. He was asked by Theodore Roosevelt, Jr., to speak at a political fund-raiser for Ogden Mills, who was running for election as a congressman from New York City.

Rogers agreed, and made a speech that was mostly jokes about the candidate. The newspapers covered the affair and his speech was featured. After that, he became a much sought after public speaker in New York. In one six-month period, he spoke sixty-one times—to trade groups, newspaper associations, testimonial dinners—anyone who asked.

He spoke his mind, and his audiences seemed to love it. He gave advice. He criticized politicians and big business. He warned against bankers. "If you think borrowing money ain't a sucker's game, why is your banker the richest man in your town?"[3] He even named names of famous financiers of the time, such as J.P. Morgan, Otto Kahn, and Charles Schwab. He told a group of bankers they were "Loan Sharks and Interest Hounds;" advertisers represented a "Lodge of Liars." However, according to his biographer, Homer Croy, later in his speech, Rogers would always tell his listeners "what fine gentlemen they were."[4]

Playing in New York with the *Follies* while his family was back in California, Rogers stayed at a hotel. He ate often at his favorite chili "joints," especially before a scheduled speech at a banquet or fund-raiser, so that he would not have to eat the banquet food. He was accumulating money now—$2,000 a week from Ziegfeld, and $20,000 for a film made in New York in which he acted as Ichabod Crane, based on Washington Irving's *The Legend of Sleepy Hollow*. The films which he had earlier produced and turned over to Pathé started to bring in some money also and he recouped most of what he had lost on them. His speaking engagements added to his income.

Will Rogers started his writing career by sending jokes to a humor magazine. Some were published. He also had published a few articles based on his *Follies* monologues of jokes and commentaries about politics. Through the help of a friend, the cartoonist Rube Goldberg, the articles reached the attention of the McNaught newspaper syndicate in 1922, and Rogers was offered a contract to write a weekly column for $500 a week. He accepted this offer and began every article with "Well, all I know is just what I read in the papers," or variations, like "As I keep the old long ears to the ground." When *The New York Times* offered to publish daily a short statement called a "squib" or "telegram" in which he stated an opinion on some topic, this assignment was easy for Will Rogers. He had no trouble dashing off a daily "squib." His brief commentary became the first item many people turned to in their daily newspapers.

While he was in New York, Betty made many cross-country train trips to see him. Sometimes the children came with her. Then, after two years of performing in the *Follies*, he went back to Hollywood in 1923 to work for Hal Roach. He joined the company of comedians hired by Roach—Harold Lloyd, Laurel and

Hardy, and the "Our Gang" players, along with many others. Rogers acted in several of Roach's "Knockabout Comedies," so called because they were filmed without a script. He said, "All I ever do on the Roach lot is run around barns and lose my pants."[5] One of the comedies he played in was his own idea, a take-off on *The Covered Wagon*, a box office success. The Will Rogers version, *Two Wagons—Both Covered*, was called by *The New York Times* "as funny as anything we have ever seen on films."[6]

With all of his media coverage, Rogers was now one of the best-known persons in the country. He had several offers to appear on stage, as well as Ziegfeld's open offer to return to the *Follies* again whenever he wished. On his last "return" in 1924, he told Ziegfeld he had to be paid more than what he formerly received. He wanted $3,000 a week (which he said other producers had offered him), plus "Transportation for myself, One Wife, Three Kids, 2 Cars, and not over 12 Horses, and a retinue of Dogs and cats."[7] He got all that he asked from Ziegfeld, and he rented a farm on Long Island where the family and the animals lived while he became the highest-paid performer in the *Follies*.

Rogers' energy never seemed to flag. He kept all his extra jobs of writing and speaking while still performing in the *Follies* and never missed a deadline. He was described as a person who did not worry, or plan too far ahead. He preferred doing things on the spur of the

Will Rogers and his children, Bill, Mary, and Jimmy, spent time together riding their favorite horses.

moment. He had no office, just a rented room in Beverly Hills to store his mail, which was mountainous. But he seldom bothered to open it, leaving that to a secretary, Daisy Tyler, who would also type his brief replies when he did not do it himself. He never kept carbon copies of any correspondence.

In 1925, Rogers returned home to California, which from then on was his home base—when he was not travelling to Europe or to Central and South America as unofficial "ambassador at large of the U.S." as the National Press Club named him.

"Aviation is not a fad, it's a necessity. . . ."[1]

—Will Rogers

Frequent Flier

Early in 1927, Will Rogers was busy giving benefit performances for flood victims in Mississippi. He was angry because Congress seemed to be delaying in providing relief for the poor people who had lost everything in the flood. He himself turned over to the Red Cross many thousands of dollars raised from the benefits. "Lord, what a blessing an organization like the Red Cross is," Rogers said. "I would rather have originated it than to have written the Constitution."[2]

On May 21, 1927, in his daily "squib" which by now appeared in over four hundred newspapers, usually on the front page, Will Rogers wrote "No attempt at jokes today."[3] He, like the rest of the nation, was intent on hearing the news about a solo airplane flight across the Atlantic, which if successful would be the first ever.

Against all odds, twenty-five-year-old Charles Lindbergh had taken off from Roosevelt Field, Long Island, for Paris. In his little specially-built monoplane, the *Spirit of St. Louis*, he was out to win the $25,000 prize offered for the first solo Atlantic flight. After thirty-three hours aloft and thirty-six hundred miles of the Atlantic Ocean behind him, he landed at LeBourget Airfield outside Paris and was mobbed by the jubilant French people.

Will Rogers became one of the modest young aviator's greatest fans. Lindbergh's success emphasized Will's conviction that air travel was the coming thing. He had moved a long way forward in his dedication to aviation since the day back in 1915 when he took his first flight on a seaplane. Some years later he was invited by United States Brigadier General "Billy" Mitchell to ride with him on an aerial view of Washington, D.C. Mitchell criticized the government's lack of preparedness in aviation, and Rogers agreed with him, noting that commercial aviation was much further advanced in Europe than in the United States. On one European trip, he took a "quick" flight from London to Moscow (two days and three stops) and he praised the convenience of plane travel.

Rogers no longer feared flying; in fact he preferred it to rail travel and began to "hop" by plane to some of his far-flung lecture tour locations. His impatience with slower travel was expressed in one of his articles, headed "On Board the California Limited, Trying to Get Out of

Kansas." He began to hire small planes and pilots for trips that would otherwise be very inconvenient, or he would fly with the mail pilots. These daring young men, who flew by the seat of their pants, reminded Rogers of the cowboys he had known. Fearless passengers like Will Rogers were allowed to fly on the airmail routes and were charged by weight as the mail was. Rogers made such flights several times. He also hired planes whenever he could. The pilots often had to make forced landings. On one trip, when the plane landed upside down, his ribs were cracked and he was badly shaken up. It did not stop him from flying again. He was always willing to take a chance. On a trip from California to Kansas City, his hired plane ran out of gas and broke a wheel when it came down in a hurry in Las Vegas, Nevada. He boarded another plane which then crashed in Cheyenne, Wyoming, but Rogers was not discouraged about continuing his flight. He grabbed a third plane and finally reached Kansas City. He could even relax in the air, write his squibs or columns, and look down on the scenery while covering great distances. Noting how many towns and villages he passed while in an airplane, Will suggested in one of his articles that towns have their names painted large on the roof-tops. In that way, barnstorming pilots could see where they were.

In June 1927, after experiencing intense stomach pain while on a lecture tour, Rogers was told by his doctor that he had to have an operation to remove his

Will Rogers (right) was a great admirer of Charles Lindbergh (left), as well as a friend.

gallstones. In those days, that was a much more serious procedure than it is today. He was critically ill for a time after the operation, and his condition was considered by his wife and his friends to be partially due to his punishing schedule, maintained for several years. Ziegfeld, who had become Rogers' friend, urged him to take a rest for three or four months from the terrible kind of life he led, which nobody else could stand. Rogers, of course, returned to his hectic schedule as soon as he got out of the hospital. Even while there he wrote his daily columns and had them mailed in on time to the newspaper editors.

By September, he was back on the job again. When he was asked to speak at a banquet in San Diego honoring Lindbergh, a few months after the famous flight, he said yes. "He is the one man in this world that I would stand on a soapbox on the corner for and try to get a peek at,"[4] Rogers said.

Will Rogers became a great admirer of Charles Lindbergh, as well as a friend. He was eager to participate in the young flier's proposed transcontinental passenger service. He was also on the list for the first transatlantic passenger flight, still a few years in the future.[5]

"A Minor League Record for Monologists. . . . back home and they liked you!"[1]

—Will Rogers

Lecture Tours

In late 1926 and for two years thereafter, in between other engagements, Will Rogers started on a lecture tour of many cities and towns across the country. Charles L. Wagner, a noted concert promoter, convinced him to do this, as there was much money to be made from such a tour. With Wagner as manager and young Bruce Quisenberry, his nineteen-year-old nephew, the son of Betty Rogers' sister, Virginia, as aide-de-camp, Rogers began the tour.

Bruce took care of box-office receipts and cleaned the ropes used in the second act of the program, in which Rogers demonstrated some of his roping tricks. Bruce was also the runner with the daily "squibs," jumping off trains to file the articles at telegraph offices along the way, sometimes having to run to get back on.

80

"The pace was grueling," he said in later years.[2] He was also part of the act in which a piano was moved off the stage. Bruce was the mover of the piano, his uncle the "helper" by picking up the piano stool, with suitable remarks. One evening, the piano collapsed in pieces, and the audience laughed, assuming it was part of the act. Rogers said, "I wish it would happen every night. . . . "[3]

He was always calm and relaxed when he was on the train, writing his daily articles as he and Bruce travelled from city to city, town to town in a crazy "zig-zagging way."[4] It seemed to Bruce that Charles Wagner took any date that was open, and then later started using a timetable to see if Will Rogers and his nephew could make it.

At first, Rogers had doubted he could hold an audience for an hour at a time. But that worry soon disappeared, as his audiences proved they would stay for as long as he would speak. In fact, he often extended his talk beyond the time allowed because the audiences wanted more. At one town, that habit of ignoring the clock cost Rogers a thousand dollars of his own money. He had to hire a special railroad car, plus engine, to take him to a scheduled performance in the next town after he missed the regular train. His lecture tour manager was often infuriated. Wagner claimed that sometimes he did not know where his client was. He thought of taking legal action against Rogers, but was advised not to by his

Will Rogers had a very busy schedule, but when he was at home, he made time for family. Rogers is shown here with his daughter Mary.

lawyer who said, "If you sue and Rogers testifies, what chance would anyone else have with a jury?"[5]

On his lecture tours, Rogers was slightly nervous right before he began his monologue. "I am always nervous," he said. "I never saw an audience that I ever faced with any confidence."[6] As soon as he launched into his "act," however, nervousness disappeared and he was completely relaxed. But the night before he was to play before three thousand people in Tulsa, Oklahoma, for the second time in his career, he was more nervous than usual. He knew that most of the audience were from his old home territory, having come in droves from Oologah and Claremore and all points around in the thirty-five miles between them and Tulsa, not to speak of friends and in-laws from Arkansas. He knew too, that they had come to see for themselves just what it was that made Willie Rogers so famous. While the group of singers that accompanied him on tour (his manager's idea) performed, he paced around backstage wondering what his old friends and neighbors were going to think of him. He wrote later, "Well, after what seemed like ages, I got started . . . and they laughed." Then he hit his stride and for two hours and fifteen minutes, he rambled on. He said, "I felt good enough that night to last me the rest of my life."[7]

Even the warm reception he received at Carnegie Hall could not exceed his success with the home folks. He tried to get out of appearing before a sophisticated

Will Rogers spent much time reading and preparing for his lectures
and appearances.

New York City audience at Carnegie Hall; he even offered to pay Charles Wagner $1,000 to cancel his date, but his manager refused to reprieve him. To Rogers' surprise, when he went onstage he received another warm reception, comparable to his welcome in "Middle America."

In all of his performances, whether in vaudeville, the *Follies* or movies, Rogers was a natural when he played some phase of himself—the bashful cowboy, the tramp, the rustic, the crackerbarrel philosopher. In his lecture appearances, he was a combination of all aspects. He enjoyed the experience of meeting so many average people. "I am out to see how America is living," he reported.[8] His lecture tours, according to biographer Ben Yagoda, "transformed Will Rogers from a vaudeville rope thrower to a national presence."[9]

Hollywood

Although Will Rogers had some close calls while flying, he was lucky enough to escape serious injury. His friend Fred Stone was not so fortunate. Stone had begun piloting his own plane. One day in 1928, he crashed and was critically injured. With both legs broken, as well as other injuries, he was unable to keep his contract to act in the Broadway musical *Three Cheers*. His daughter Dorothy Stone was to co-star with him. When Rogers heard the bad news, he decided at once to take his friend's place in the show even though he would have to disrupt a lecture tour. He told Stone he would "plug along till you are able to rejoin," and "I will do the best I can with the part."[2] He joined the show with only two weeks to rehearse Stone's part. He was an immediate hit with the Broadway audiences as well as all the theater critics. They said that although Will Rogers acted as himself, no one could match him in timing, technique, humor, and rapport with his audience. He made *Three Cheers* "the hottest ticket in town" and the "last chance to see Will Rogers on Broadway."[3]

Rogers put on a different performance each evening, often adding more talk to his part, thus lengthening the play's time. The audience loved it, although the theater's manager did not always appreciate the unexpected additions. As usual, Rogers was taking matters into his own hands.

After he completed a successful run of *Three Cheers*, he returned home—again—to California, ready to begin the next phase of his career—acting in talking pictures. This was called by one of Rogers' biographers the "most significant professional move of the rest of his life."[4] However, he himself did not hesitate to call the movie business "cuckoo," and say that the only thing that would hurt it is "when the people in movies or going to them ever start taking them seriously."[5]

Ever since 1923, the moving picture producers had been trying to synchronize sound with moving images on film. By 1928, they succeeded, and the "talkies" were born.

The stars of the old silent films had to learn how to speak when they acted. Some managed to survive in the new medium. Othedrs, like Pola Negri, Clara Bow, and John Gilbert were found to lack good voices for the "talkies." Of all the winners, Will Rogers headed the list. He was a natural for talking pictures, the man they were invented for, it was said.[6] He came across much more forcefully than in his silent films. His voice was strong, his style natural, his drawl authentic, part of his personality.

In 1929, he signed a contract with Fox, and the company's production chief, Winfield Sheehan, to make four talking motion pictures for $600,000. He had started his second career in movies: "a new level of fame and financial security."[7] His first film, *They Had to See Paris,* "fitted Will" it was said, "like a pair of twenty-five year old overalls."[8] He played a plain Oklahoman whose oil well turned his family into rich, "high society" snobs, until he brought them back down to earth.

Like his acts onstage or in his speeches, Rogers' success in talking pictures was largely due to what he said and how he said it. Talking held no terrors for him, he was never at a loss for words, on the set or off. After his first contract with Fox ran out, he signed others that kept him with the same movie company for the rest of his life. Some of his better-known films were: *A Connecticut Yankee, Judge Priest, Life Begins at Forty, State Fair,* and *Steamboat 'Round the Bend.* Among his many co-stars were Mickey Rooney, Slim Summerville, Myrna Loy, Andy Devine, Stepin Fetchit, and Irvin Cobb. By the early 1930s, he was number one on the list of box office attractions, ahead of other famous performers like Mae West, Joan Crawford, and Clark Gable.

He never attended the previews of his films, or the parties that were held afterward. The Hollywood scene, often wild and sensational, was not for him. (Even in his films, the love interest was played down.) Although he had leading roles, his parts were always some version of himself. Will Rogers movies were never censored by those who rated motion pictures on moral standards. He himself would be the first to uphold wholesome qualities in films. He said he would never "make a movie that parents didn't want their children to see."[9]

As soon as he had begun to make "big" money from acting in the movies, Will Rogers made several investments in California real estate. He advised one young friend, actor Joel McCrea, to do the same. Rogers bought some ocean front land for $20,000; he later sold it to William Randolph Hearst, the newspaper mogul, for $100,000. He kept buying more land, his chief form of investment along with life insurance. It all came to over a million dollars, with the interest amounting to many thousands annually. However, he was by now the highest-paid movie actor in Hollywood and he could afford his expensive investments. Luckily for him, he did not put money in the stock market. When the market crashed in 1929, and brought about the financial ruin of many people he knew, Will Rogers was secure.

One of his big investments was the three hundred

acres of land in the Santa Monica hills where he planned to build his ideal ranch. In the beginning, the property had only a small log cabin which the family used as a weekend retreat when they wanted to get away from Beverly Hills. Then, as plans for his new ranch grew more elaborate, Rogers hired his brother-in-law, Lee Adamson, the husband of Betty's sister Anne, to supervise the construction of a bigger house and all the outbuildings for horses and calves.

He himself could not be on the spot while his plans were carried out, so he sent letters to Adamson, and also to his own family, even his son Jimmy, with instructions about what he wanted them to do. He told twelve-year-old Jimmy to check on some aspects of the stables being built for their many horses. "Get 'em to build the back part on the big barn. . . . move the old Stables," he wrote.[10] When completed the stables were enormous, so magnificient that visitors to the ranch teased Will for having a more splendid "barn" as he called the stables, than his house.

When not making films, Rogers was on the lecture tours which also earned big money for him. He liked to make money, and he did, over his lifetime, make a great deal. But he spent freely, too, not only on property, but on travel (he paid his own expenses), his family, his horses and calves, and the needs of his friends and relatives. His own wants were simple, and the help he gave to others was never mentioned by him.

Will Rogers spent his money freely, including buying this new car.

When Colonel Mulhall, old and ill, fell on hard times, Rogers met him on a visit to Oklahoma. Before leaving, he pressed a large wad of bills into the old man's hand. Florenz Ziegfeld was wiped out financially in the stock market crash of 1929. He came to California to live and often visited the Rogers family at the ranch. He died in 1932, and Rogers paid the medical bills and funeral expenses of his old "boss." Any friend from the early days in Oklahoma who asked for his help received it, including the cowboys and farm hands.

By 1928, the new ranch house was ready for year-round residence. The family moved from their home in Beverly Hills into the place that would be their homestead. It was a real, western-style house, although as Rogers said, "very plain and ordinary, all on one floor." The property was not a ranch by Texas standards, but according to him, "Everything out here [California] that is not an apartment is a ranch. We even call mine a ranch, and there's nothing on it but an old polo field, a few calves to rope, and some old cow ponies."[11]

Things were brought from his home in Oologah to furnish the house, like the lighting fixture made from an old wagon wheel. Other items were picked up on Rogers' travels or given to him by friends—saddles, spurs, branding irons, and a stuffed calf, the gift of his artist friend Ed Burein, to enable him to practice roping indoors. Surrounding the house were the stables, a roping ring, a polo field, a tennis court, and a small golf

The living room of Rogers' western-style house showed his tastes to be simple, despite his wealth.

course for the use of friends. Rogers did not play golf himself. He said if he did, it would have to be on a horse. Sometimes there were as many as thirty polo horses in the stables. As the Rogers sons grew older, they played with him. Other horses were used for roping; many were strays that Rogers had adopted. Betty Rogers said, "From the size of our feed bill you would have thought we were an orphanage for all the stray horses in the United States."[12] Rogers' most cherished horses were Soapsuds for roping and Bootlegger for polo. Small, but very fast and quick in turning, Bootlegger was a beautiful little horse, with mane and tail flowing free, unlike most of the other polo ponies whose manes and tails were cropped. Rogers would not have that done to Bootlegger, and people who visited the ranch always remembered "the little black pony and what a beautiful sight he was, with his long mane and tail standing out stiff in the wind, as he and Will came flying down the field."[13]

There were always calves on hand, too, most of them for roping, which Rogers practiced every day that he was at the ranch. One of them was called Sarah, after Sarah Kleberg, a good friend who owned the vast Kleberg ranch in Texas. She had given the valuable Brahman calf to the Rogers family, and the animal soon became a household pet, always appearing whenever the family went outside to sit, curling up contentedly at their feet.

On Sundays when Rogers was at home, he invited

friends to the ranch to play polo with him. Some of the many guests who came were Rogers' old friends Fred Stone and Tom Mix, and actors Spencer Tracy, Leslie Howard, and a young cowboy actor who later changed his name from Leonard Slye to Roy Rogers because of his admiration for Will Rogers. Besides playing polo with his friends, Rogers' greatest pleasures, according to biographer Homer Croy, were his "family, travel, roping calves, going visiting, . . . [and] swapping stories."[14]

The two older Rogers children were in their teens when the family moved to the Santa Monica ranch. As youngsters, all three had been given music and dancing lessons, as well as riding and horsemanship instruction from their father. As they approached college age, their interests diverged. Will Rogers, Jr., the oldest, entered Stanford University after a summer spent working for the *Fort Worth Texas Star-Telegram*. He was interested in writing and politics. Mary Rogers wanted to be an actress, although her father tried to dissuade her from movie acting. Once, when he was pestered by a woman trying to get her young child in the movies, Rogers told his children, "I'm glad you don't have any talent."[15] After a year at Sarah Lawrence College, Mary took a job playing in summer stock and she continued this for a few years. She used the name Mary Howard, not wishing to capitalize on her father's fame. Jim Rogers, the youngest child, was very much like his father in his love of horses and riding. He was the "cowboy son." As a youngster, Jim played the same kind of practical jokes as his father had done before him. He and a cousin once tied a string of firecrackers to the tail of a steer Rogers used in his roping demonstrations. When the steer charged out to be roped, the firecrackers went off, scaring steer, horse, and rider. "Dad never did catch that steer," Jim said. "I didn't go near the house for days as long as he was there."[16]

Rogers, as his children knew, had a quick temper and a short fuse. He was impatient when he was teaching them to ride and rope.[17] Discipline was considered to be Betty's job. She did it when necessary, and maintained the simple, unpretentious style of living that she and her husband preferred. She said once, "Our parents were wholesome country people and that's the kind of life we like. And the kind we want our children to like."[18]

In the beginning, Betty was away from home a great deal too, traveling with her husband. She had to decide early in her marriage whether to remain home with the children or to accompany Will on his tours. She decided that Will needed her more. He depended on her to keep his life and business matters on a regulated basis. He was known to have carried several uncashed paychecks in his pockets for weeks, and Betty, as she said, learned to control the family purse strings. While both parents were away, Betty's sister Theda Blake stayed with the children. Both Will Rogers and Betty wanted them to have the maternal care that he had missed as a child after his

The Rogers family's happiest times were when they were all on the ranch together. The family is shown here at their Santa Monica ranch.

mother died. So Aunt Theda became the Rogers children's second mother. She was a permanent member of the household when they were young, along with Paula McSpadden, Rogers' niece, the daughter of his sister Sallie, who was the youngsters' companion on outings to plays, picnics, and ballgames.

Yet the Rogers family's happiest times were when they were all on the ranch together. After the vaudeville years were over, Betty stayed home, and when she did travel to wherever Rogers was performing, the children often came with her. The rest of the time, they waited for him to come home and, hopefully, stay for awhile. Mary, especially, missed her father when he was away. As a young woman, she once told actor Joel McCrea, "You know, we resent you a little bit. You take up so much of our father's time."[19]

Life on the ranch was relaxed and casual when Will Rogers was at home. He wore his usual costume—blue jeans, boots, a cowboy shirt, and a bandanna around his neck. His ever-present Stetson hat was almost always on his head. He never wore the wide-brimmed cowboy hat that so many other Hollywood actors affected. On tours, he wore a sober blue serge suit, a white shirt, and a black bow tie. When on shipboard with his family, he made the boys—young men by that time—wear tuxedos, although he himself never did.

"After acting a Fool all over the World and part of Iowa, I have been back home, and they seemed glad to see me. . . "[1]
—Will Rogers

On the Go

Will Rogers always seemed to be "on the go." His lifelong wanderlust, his curiosity about new places, new things, never left him. One of his biographers said that he was "fiddle-footed;" as his son Jim put it, "he just had to see what was on the other side of every mountain in the world."[2] Even at home, on his beloved ranch, he was not content to stay there very long. If he had a week's lay-off from making Hollywood movies, he would fly to New York, or go back home to Claremore and spend the time visiting relatives and friends. That was when he would get real Oklahoma home cooking at his sisters' home—navy beans, fried ham, cream gravy, and corn pone.

He traveled to Europe several times, sometimes alone, on the spur of the moment, sometimes with Betty and the children. Accompanied by war correspondent Floyd Gibbons, he got close to some danger spots in Asia. He wrote that the war between Japan and Manchuria was "a better fight to keep out of."[3] He flew across India. He visited Hong Kong, Singapore, Cairo, and Baghdad. Whenever Betty was with him, they toured the continent of Europe. Every trip convinced Rogers of America's superiority and the need for this country to keep out of foreign entanglements that could lead to war. A magazine quote expressed the influence Will Rogers exerted on so many people. "You can never have another war in this country unless Will Rogers is for it."[4]

Although Rogers was loved and admired by millions of Americans, he did have his detractors, among them the critic H. L. Mencken, who said, "I consider him the most dangerous writer alive today."[5] When Rogers replied that nobody with any sense took his gags seriously, Mencken retorted that "They are taken seriously by nobody except half-wits, in other words by 85 percent of the voting population."[6] In spite of those remarks, Mencken and Will Rogers considered themselves friends.

Rogers did not hesitate to ridicule politicians, but many would not take him on publicly, knowing his great appeal to the common people. The mayor of Chicago may not have considered that when he called Rogers "a wisecracker . . . the cheapest skate on earth," but the fact remains that the mayor lost his election the following year.[7]

Claiming that he was always for the "Big Honest Majority of Americans," Will Rogers was also for the farmers and the underdogs; against stock market speculation, and buying on credit.[8] He favored a strong military, especially in the air, because he predicted another world war.

From the beginning, Congress was a favorite target for many of his jokes. He called Congress the "National Joke Factory,"[9] and had said when he was performing in the *Follies*, "I am to go into Ziegfeld's *Follies*, and I have no act. So I run down to Washington and get some material," and, he continued, "Congress is good enough for me. They have been writing my material for years . . . I am going to stick to them."[10] Compared to those in Congress, he said, "I'm an amateur."[11]

Although he criticized Congress and gave it free advice, he had many friends of both parties there, especially those from his part of the country— Oklahoma, Texas, and Arkansas. He was on good terms with all the Presidents he lived under, except Warren Harding and Herbert Hoover. He liked New York Governor Al Smith, who tried but never won the presidency, and admired Franklin Roosevelt, who did.

Rogers began attending the political party conventions in 1924 and he continued "kidding" them every four years after that. He poked fun at the foolishness he saw at the raucous, rowdy meetings. "Those that are in are trying to stay in, and those that are out are trying to get in," he said.[12] He declared that the nominating speeches were pure "applesauce," and should be eliminated, leaving nothing but flags and bands. After all, he said, "our National Conventions are nothing but glorified Mickey Mouse cartoons . . . solely for amusement purposes."[13]

He joined in the fun when the magazine *Life* nominated him as leader of the Anti-Bunk Party. Rogers said that left him dazed but "If I stay dazed, I ought to make a splendid candidate."[14] Although he claimed to be a Democrat, he made jokes about both national parties. He said that the Republicans took credit for such things as "radio, telephones, baths, automobiles, savings accounts, workmen living in houses, and a living wage for senators." The Democrats, according to the Republicans, he said, had brought on "War, pestilence, debts, Disease, Bo[ll] weevil, Gold teeth, need of Farm relief, suspenders, floods, famines."[15]

Will Rogers himself was the choice of what was unofficially called the "Great Silent Vote," but when in 1928, his name was put up as a candidate for President—not altogether as a joke—he was disturbed by the fact that people would seriously consider him for high office. He said it was "pathetic to think of a professional comedian as president."[16] He had left Oklahoma, he said, because if he stayed there he would

102

have to work, and that is what he always avoided. His job was kidding people. He suspected, he said, that people would sooner or later, "catch onto him."[17] Then he and Betty would go back to Claremore, where he had purchased thirty acres as a possible site for their future home. In the meantime, he would continue doing what he was doing; he attributed his success to luck or accident.

In the several books by Will Rogers that were published, the spelling and grammar were left just as he had originally written them. After one of his first, *The Illiterate Digest* rose high on the best-seller lists, publishers wanted more of Will Rogers in book form. He responded by putting together selections from his articles and columns. Examples of his output were *The Cowboy Philosopher* series, and a volume based on his Russian experiences, called *There's Not a Bathing Suit in Russia*. On his trip to the Soviet Union in 1925, Rogers was refused permission to interview Leon Trotsky, the leader of the Russian revolution in 1917. He realized that the authorities were keeping Trotsky under wraps, for which he was sorry because "I have never yet met a man that I dident [sic] like."[18] That became one of his most famous sayings, repeated several times in his writing and speaking. In 1930, he even said that his epitaph should read "I joked about every prominent man of my time, but I never met a man I dident [sic] like."[19]

The more well known Will Rogers became, the more

he was admired. He became as popular on radio as *Amos 'n Andy*. He had big commercial sponsors for his radio talks; one was the Squibb Pharmaceutical Company, who paid him $77,000 in 1930 for a series of short speeches. As *The New York Times* noted, that was as much as the great Babe Ruth's annual salary.

Rogers was always conscious of the hard times many Americans experienced after the stock market crash in 1929. The depression that followed in the early 1930s worried him, especially unemployment. In 1931, 15 million people were out of work.[20] When the Gulf Oil Company sponsored him in a series of broadcasts, he donated all of his $50,000 fee to unemployment relief. That was to be administered through the two agencies he contributed to throughout his life—the Salvation Army and the Red Cross.

Franklin D. Roosevelt was elected President in 1932, and Will Rogers was confident that the New Deal would result in better times for the American people. He praised President Roosevelt, and Eleanor Roosevelt, the First Lady, also, because she was fair-minded and paid her way when she traveled on regular passenger planes.[21]

When Rogers was asked by the editor of the *Saturday Evening Post* to write the story of his life, he started on the project, but did not get far. After two years, he notified the editor that he was sorry the book was not ready. He could not say when it would be ready, but

Will Rogers (left) had many well-known friends, including actress Billie Burke, aviator Wiley Post, and actor Fred Stone.

he added to his apology a note "the longer I live the more life you get all at original price."[22] It was clear that he did not care to write about himself, nor talk about himself.

His autobiography did not come out until several years after his death.

". . . nothing that I have ever seen is more beautiful than this inland passage . . . to Alaska."[1]

—Will Rogers

Last Journey

In 1934, Will and Betty Rogers and their two sons went on an around-the-world trip. Will Rogers, Jr., was twenty-three, Jim was nineteen. Mary, twenty-one, would not join the group, as she was playing in summer stock in Maine. The journey began in San Francisco, where the family boarded a ship bound for Honolulu. From there, the Rogers party went to Japan, Korea, and then Russia. They rode on a Trans-Siberian Railroad train that took eight days to reach Moscow. Cooped up in a tiny compartment, Rogers longed for an airplane view of the vast, wild country that he said reminded him of Indian Territory when he was growing up.

After Russia came Scandinavia, Austria, the Balkans, the rest of Europe, and at last, the British Isles. From there, Will and Betty returned home, while their two sons went on to Paris. As a result of his trip, Rogers professed hope for world peace. But in March 1935, when actions taken by Hitler and Mussolini defied the peace treaties and foretold the growth of fascism, he could see only the looming disaster of a second world war.

In the spring of 1934, Rogers had scored another hit in show business. He played the lead in the West Coast production of Eugene O'Neill's play *Ah, Wilderness*. He was a great success, but he left the role when a minister wrote to him declaring that the play was improper for family viewing. Rogers took that opinion seriously, and as a result, won release from his contract to play the same role in the movie version, thereby losing over $200,000. In today's money, that would be close to $2 million.

In early summer, 1935, after finishing his last movie, *Steamboat 'Round the Bend*, Rogers had some free time. All he had to do was to write his articles and telegrams. There were no scheduled tours or benefit shows for a while. Yet, as usual, he was restless. "I've got to travel," he said whenever people asked him why he did not stay home. "I've got to go places . . . to see things to talk about."[2] He was thinking of another long trip. Maybe he and Betty would go to Rio de Janeiro and board the *Graf Zeppelin*, the dirigible that was making regularly scheduled flights from South America to Europe. Then Wiley Post came to see him. That visit changed all of the previous plans.

Wiley Post was one of the best-known aviators in the country. In 1931, when he was thirty-two, he flew around the world with his navigator, Harold Getty, in eight days. Two years later, he did it again, in seven days, alone in his small plane, the *Winnie Mae.* Post also tried several times to reach the stratosphere and break the existing altitude record of forty-seven thousand feet.

Will Rogers and Wiley Post had met several years before, at the Oklahoma City airport. Fellow Oklahomans, they became friends. The young pilot had bought his own plane when he was only eighteen, with the compensation he received for losing an eye in an accident while working for an oil company. After that, the eye patch he always wore became a distinguishing feature. Will Rogers followed Wiley Post's achievements with great interest. Early in 1935, Post was busy assembling a special new plane from parts of other planes. He planned to fly to Alaska that summer to survey the possibility of a mail route to Russia, via Siberia. He added pontoons to his plane because of the possibility of landing on lagoons in Alaska. Post asked Rogers if he wanted to go along, and his friend was definitely interested. Rogers had never been to Alaska, and he was keen on seeing Siberia from the air.

Betty Rogers was not enthusiastic about her husband's going on such a trip, but when she heard that Wiley Post was to be the pilot, she felt better about the undertaking. Until just a few days before leaving, Rogers himself was not wholly committed about going. He knew Betty was not happy about it, especially about the plan to go on the long dangerous flight over Siberia after leaving Alaska. She said later, "Will wanted me to want him to go. . . . And so I tried to be happy about this."[3]

On the afternoon of the day he was to leave, as Rogers was packing his bag, he called Betty, "Say, Blake, you know what I just did? I flipped a coin." When Betty came in the room she said she hoped it came out tails; he laughed and held out his hand. "No, it didn't. It's heads. See, I win."[4]

He promised Betty that he would call her from Alaska before taking off for Russia. The plans for continuing the flight would be reconsidered when the fliers reached Nome. Rogers joined Wiley Post in Seattle, Washington, on August 6, 1935, and they took off on the thousand mile hop to Juneau, Alaska. Everything went well, and in Juneau there was a meeting with an old friend, writer Rex Beach, and the well-known Alaska bush pilot, Joe Crosson. They all talked well into the night. Rogers sent off his daily telegrams in one of which he said, "This Alaska is a great country."[5] He and Wiley Post resumed their journey and made their way steadily north, from Juneau to Yukon Territory, then to the Northwest Territory. They stopped at Fairbanks. There they stayed for a few days while Rogers typed out and mailed four weekly articles. From Fairbanks he sent a telegram to his daughter,

Mary, telling her not to worry and to send any wires to him at Nome. When Betty saw that—she had already reached Maine where she planned a visit with Mary—she knew that he had decided to go to Russia with Wiley Post because Nome was the taking off point for Siberia.

First however, Rogers wanted to visit Barrow, the northernmost part of Alaska, although it was not on the way to Nome, and meant an extra five hundred mile journey from Fairbanks over mountains and lagoons. Charlie Brower, a legendary old trader and trapper who lived in Barrow, was the object of his desire to go there. Brower would provide good material for a newspaper column. As Rogers was paying the expenses, Wiley Post agreed to take the side trip to Barrow. The weather was not promising, and when Joe Crosson learned of the planned flight, he advised against it because of the heavy fog covering the region. After two days in Fairbanks, as the fog persisted, Wiley Post grew impatient and told his passenger, "I think we can make it." Rogers said, "If it's good enough for you, it's good enough for me."[6] As Post had told Joe Crosson, they would proceed by contact flying—keeping the ground in sight. They took off, but before the fog lifted enough to see the ground, Post had lost his way, taking wrong turns then circling around without being able to spot their destination. Finally, after several hours, the fog cleared somewhat and Post touched down on a small lagoon, near a tiny settlement

On a stop in Alaska, Will Rogers (standing on airplane) waited while
pilot Wiley Post signed an autograph.

he could see from the air. A few Eskimos approached the plane, and one of them, Clare Okpeaha, knew a little English. He told the two fliers that Barrow was not far away and pointed in its direction. Wiley Post and Will Rogers climbed back in the plane and took off. As the Eskimos watched, the plane rose, banked, and then the engine failed. The plane dove straight down into the lagoon and crashed.

Clare Okpeaha ran as close as he could get to the fallen plane and called out several times. There was no answer. He immediately started to Barrow, the nearest place where an outpost was maintained. Running over rain-soaked ground, it took him less than two hours to reach Barrow. When he described the two men who had crashed in their plane, the American authorities at the outpost realized with dismay that it must be Wiley Post and Will Rogers. Three motor boats and a umiak, a rowboat used for towing were put in the water. Then with a crew of Eskimos, and Clare Okpeaha, three of the Americans from the outpost went to the scene of the accident. When they arrived, they saw there was no hope for finding the plane's passengers alive. The bodies were placed in the umiak, and then the men made the slow, sorrowful journey back to Barrow. Those who awaited them knew that the worst had happened when they heard the throttled-down engine motors and the Eskimos chanting their mournful song for the dead.

What had caused the accident? There were two

theories advanced by the experts and others who examined the plane at the scene of the crash. One theory was that the pontoons Post had attached to the plane made it nose-heavy, difficult to climb. The other theory was that having lost his way in the fog, by the time he landed near the Eskimos, Post had run out of gas. He would have been able to refuel at Barrow.

When the news of the crash was sent around the world, there was widespread shock and mourning. Will Rogers was the subject of eulogies all over the land. Repeated over and over was the line from Shakespeare: "We shall not look upon his like again."[7]

The bodies of the two men were flown back to the mainland by Joe Crosson. On the day of Will Rogers' funeral, fifty thousand people filed by his casket in Forest Lawn Memorial Park in Los Angeles. At the same time, memorial services were held all over the country. All the motion picture studios were closed. In New York City theaters were darkened. The radio networks observed a half hour of silence. Flags were at half mast; planes flying overhead dipped their wings in salute.

There is a majestic memorial to Will Rogers, dedicated in 1938, in Claremore, where Will Rogers is now buried, along with his wife, who died nine years after him, baby Fred, their youngest child, and Mary, who died in 1989. Before Betty Rogers died, she left the Santa Monica ranch to the state of California. It is known now as the Will Rogers State Historical Park.

A statue of Will Rogers by the noted sculptor Jo Davidson stands at the Claremore Memorial. It is inscribed with Rogers' famous statement, "I never met a man I didn't like." A duplicate of that statue is in Statuary Hall in the United States Capitol in Washington, D.C., where all the states in the union are represented by statues of their foremost citizens. Will Rogers stands not only for Oklahoma, but for the entire nation.

Over the years since his death in 1935, the name of Will Rogers has faded somewhat from Americans' memory. In the 1990s, there has been a growing recognition of him as "a man of the people, a symbol of his time."[8] He is remembered today as someone who reflected and recorded the life and times of an era with clarity, compassion, and humor.

Chronology

1879—On November 4, William Penn Adair Rogers (Will Rogers) is born near Oologah, Indian Territory, now Oklahoma.

1887—Attends several schools in Indian Territory and
-1898 Missouri.

1898—Works as a cowboy on the Ewing ranch in Texas.

1899—Manages the Rogers ranch after father, Clem
-1902 Rogers, moves to Claremore, Oklahoma.

1902—Leaves for South America; works and performs
-1904 in Wild West shows and circuses in South Africa, Australia, and New Zealand.

1904—Joins Colonel Zack Mulhall's troupe of
-1905 musicians and cowboys.

1905—Begins vaudeville career; travels on the
-1908 vaudeville circuit.

1908—Marries Betty Blake at her family home in Arkansas on November 23.

1911—Will and Betty Rogers' first son, Will Rogers, Jr., is born in New York City; Clem Rogers dies.

1912—Appears in Broadway musical comedy *The Wall Street Girl.*

1913—Daughter, Mary Amelia Rogers, born in Arkansas.

1915—Second son, James Blake Rogers, born on Long Island, New York; Will Rogers joins Ziegfeld's *Midnight Frolic;* takes first flight on seaplane.

1916— Performs as star of *Ziegfeld Follies*.
-1919

1917— Holds wartime benefits for the American forces in World War I; contributes generously to Red Cross.

1918— Third son, Fred Stone Rogers, born on Long Island; Will Rogers makes his first silent movie, *Laughing Bill Hyde*.

1919— Begins publishing weekly newspaper articles, books, and daily squibs; moves to California to act in silent movies.

1920— Baby Fred Rogers dies at twenty months; family settles in Beverly Hills, their home for next ten years.

1922— Will Rogers produces his own movies; the company fails and Rogers goes back to the *Follies* to regain money lost.

1923— Returns to California to work for Hal Roach, producer of short silent comedies; starts career as popular public speaker.

1924— Covers both political party conventions; continues writing, speaking, publishing books: One of best known, *The Illiterate Digest*, becomes best-seller.

1925— Takes airplane ride with General "Billy" Mitchell, aviation sponsor; becomes an aviation enthusiast; leaves *Follies* for good.

1927— Has surgery and is hospitalized; visits Mexico
-1928   and meets Charles Lindbergh; travels on second lecture tour across the country.

1928—Covers national conventions; takes Fred Stone's place in musical comedy *Three Cheers*.

1929—Makes first talking picture, *They Had to See Paris*; signs contract to make four films a year.

1930—Delivers first radio broadcast sponsored by E. R. Squibb.

1931—Holds benefit performances for drought victims, earthquake survivors, and other causes; broadcasts for Gulf Oil Company; fee donated to charity; travels to Asia.

1932—Florenz Ziegfeld dies; Will Rogers delivers eulogy; travels all over South America by plane; attends national political conventions.

1933—Continues radio broadcasts, movies, newspaper articles; master of ceremonies for Academy Awards.

1934—Plays leading role in Eugene O'Neill's *Ah, Wilderness*; takes trip around the world with his family.

1935—Leaves on airplane trip to Alaska with Wiley Post; August 15, plane crashes not far from Barrow; Will Rogers and Wiley Post are killed instantly; memorial services are held throughout the country.

Chapter Notes

Chapter 1

1. Donald Day, *Will Rogers: A Biography* (New York: McKay, 1962), p. 90.

2. Ibid., p. 85.

3. Ibid., p. 80.

4. Richard M. Ketchum, *Will Rogers: His Life and Times* (New York: American Heritage, 1973), p. 150.

5. Ben Yagoda, *Will Rogers: A Biography* (New York: Alfred A. Knopf, 1993), p. 146.

Chapter 2

1. Will Rogers, *The Autobiography of Will Rogers* (Boston: Houghton Mifflin, 1949), p. 5.

2. Betty Rogers, *Will Rogers: His Wife's Story* (Indianapolis: Bobbs-Merrill, 1941), p. 29.

3. Richard M. Ketchum, *Will Rogers: His Life and Times* (New York: American Heritage, 1973), p. 38.

4. Ibid.

5. Ibid.

Chapter 3

1. Will Rogers, *The Autobiography of Will Rogers* (Boston: Houghton Mifflin, 1949), p. 5.

2. Richard M. Ketchum, *Will Rogers: His Life and Times* (New York: American Heritage, 1973), p. 39.

3. Ben Yagoda, *Will Rogers: A Biography* (New York: Alfred A. Knopf, 1993), p. 24.

4. Ibid., p. 25.

5. Spi M. Trent, *My Cousin Will Rogers* (New York: Putnam, 1938), p. 41.

Chapter 4

1. Will Rogers, *The Autobiography of Will Rogers* (Boston: Houghton Mifflin, 1949), p. 12.

2. Bryan B. Sterling, *The Will Rogers Scrapbook* (New York: Grosset and Dunlap, 1976), p. 16.

3. Richard M. Ketchum, *Will Rogers: His Life and Times* (New York: American Heritage, 1973), p. 83.

4. Spi M. Trent, *My Cousin Will Rogers* (New York: Putnam, 1938), p. 155.

5. Ketchum, p. 61.

6. Trent, p. 73.

7. Ben Yagoda, *Will Rogers: A Biography* (New York: Alfred A. Knopf, 1993), p. 47.

8. Ibid.

9. Ibid., p. 39.

10. Trent, pp. 108–109.

11. Yagoda, p. 40.

12. Ibid.

13. Ketchum, p. 114.

14. Yagoda, p. 47.

Chapter 5

1. Will Rogers, *The Autobiography of Will Rogers* (Boston: Houghton Mifflin, 1949), p. 23.

2. Ibid., p. 17.

3. Donald Day, *Will Rogers: A Biography* (New York: McKay, 1962), p. 42.

4. Rogers, p. 19.

5. Betty Rogers, *Will Rogers: His Wife's Story* (Indianapolis: Bobbs-Merrill, 1941), p. 77.

6. Ibid., p. 75.

7. Ibid., p. 78.

8. Homer Croy, *Our Will Rogers* (New York: Duell, Sloan and Pearce, 1953), p. 86.

9. Richard M. Ketchum, *Will Rogers: His Life and Times* (New York: American Heritage, 1973), p. 85.

Chapter 6

1. Will Rogers, *The Autobiography of Will Rogers* (Boston: Houghton Mifflin, 1949), pp. 30–31.

2. Richard M. Ketchum, *Will Rogers: His Life and Times* (New York: American Heritage, 1973), p. 92.

3. Ben Yagoda, *Will Rogers: A Biography* (New York: Alfred A. Knopf, 1993), p. 77.

4. Ibid.

5. Ibid., p. 82.

6. Ketchum, p. 108.

7. Ibid., p. 109.

8. Ibid., p. 113.

9. Ibid.

10. Ibid.

11. Ibid., p. 128.

12. Ibid., p. 127.

13. Ibid., pp. 127–128.

Chapter 7

1. Will Rogers, *The Autobiography of Will Rogers* (Boston: Houghton Mifflin, 1949), p. 35.

2. Richard M. Ketchum, *Will Rogers: His Life and Times* (New York: American Heritage, 1973), pp. 123–124.

3. Ben Yagoda, *Will Rogers: A Biography* (New York: Alfred A. Knopf, 1993), p. 271.

4. Ibid., p. 127.

5. Ketchum, p. 175.

6. Ibid., p. 126.

7. Ibid.

Chapter 8

1. Will Rogers, *The Autobiography of Will Rogers* (Boston: Houghton Mifflin, 1949), p. 137.

2. Bryan B. Sterling and Frances N. Sterling, *A Will Rogers Treasury* (New York: Crown, 1982), p. 243.

3. Ibid.

4. Richard M. Ketchum, *Will Rogers: His Life and Times* (New York: American Heritage, 1973), p. 137.

5. Donald Day, *Will Rogers: A Biography* (New York: McKay, 1962), p. 115.

6. Ibid., p. 93.

7. Ben Yagoda, *Will Rogers: A Biography* (New York: Alfred A. Knopf, 1993), p. 143.

8. Ibid.

9. Ketchum, p. 150.

Chapter 9

1. Will Rogers, *The Autobiography of Will Rogers* (Boston: Houghton Mifflin, 1949), p. 81.

2. Richard M. Ketchum, *Will Rogers: His Life and Times* (New York: American Heritage, 1973), p. 165.

3. Homer Croy, *Our Will Rogers* (New York: Duell, Sloan and Pearce, 1953), p. 168.

4. Ibid.

5. Ben Yagoda, *Will Rogers: A Biography* (New York: Alfred A. Knopf, 1993), p. 206.

6. Ibid.

7. Ibid., p. 209.

Chapter 10

1. Will Rogers, *The Autobiography of Will Rogers* (Boston: Houghton Mifflin, 1949), p. 201.

2. Donald Day, *Will Rogers: A Biography* (New York: McKay, 1962), p. 209.

3. Rogers, p. 149.

4. Ben Yagoda, *Will Rogers: A Biography* (New York: Alfred A. Knopf, 1993), p. 243.

5. Ibid., p. 244.

Chapter 11

1. Ben Yagoda, *Will Rogers: A Biography* (New York: Alfred A. Knopf, 1993), p. 223.

2. Ibid., p. 225.

3. Ibid., p. 227.

4. Ibid., p. 225.

5. Ibid., p. 254.

6. Richard M. Ketchum, *Will Rogers: His Life and Times* (New York: American Heritage, 1973), p. 175.

7. Yagoda, p. 223.

8. Ibid., p. 222.

9. Ibid., p. 223.

Chapter 12

1. Will Rogers, *The Autobiography of Will Rogers* (Boston: Houghton Mifflin, 1949), p. 97.

2. Richard M. Ketchum, *Will Rogers: His Life and Times* (New York: American Heritage, 1973), p. 252.

3. Ben Yagoda, *Will Rogers: A Biography* (New York: Alfred A. Knopf, 1993), p. 255.

4. Ibid.

5. Steve K. Gragert, *Will Rogers Weekly Articles*, Vol. 4 (Stillwater, Okla.: Oklahoma State University Press, 1981), p. 307.

6. Yagoda, p. 259.

7. Ibid., p. 260.

8. Ibid., p. 261.

9. Ketchum, p. 257.

10. Ibid., p. 222.

11. Gragert, p. 157.

12. Donald Day, *Will Rogers: A Biography* (New York: McKay, 1962), p. 258.

13. Ketchum, p. 306.

14. Homer Croy, *Our Will Rogers* (New York: Duell, Sloan and Pearce, 1953), p. 230.

15. Ketchum, p. 307.

16. Gragert, p. 309.

17. Ketchum, p. 306.

18. Ibid., p. 307.

19. Yagoda, p. 276

Chapter 13

1. Will Rogers, *The Autobiography of Will Rogers* (Boston: Houghton Mifflin, 1949), pp. 119–120.

2. Ben Yagoda, *Will Rogers: A Biography* (New York: Alfred A. Knopf, 1993), p. 276.

3. Ibid., p. 278.

4. Ibid., p. 292.

5. Ibid., p. 288.

6. Ibid.

7. Ibid., p. 292.

8. Rogers, p. xvi.

9. Donald Day, *Will Rogers: A Biography* (New York: McKay, 1962), p. 145.

10. Bryan B. Sterling, *The Will Rogers Scrapbook* (New York: Grosset & Dunlap, 1976), p. 110.

11. Ibid., p. 111.

12. Richard M. Ketchum, *Will Rogers: His Life and Times* (New York: American Heritage, 1973), p. 243.

13. Sterling, p. 110.

14. Ketchum, p. 244.

15. Ibid., p. 247.

16. Yagoda, p. 251.

17. Ketchum, p. 317.

18. Yagoda, p. 234.

19. Ibid.

20. Ketchum, p. 323.

21. Ibid., p. 335.

22. Yagoda, p. 216.

Chapter 14

1. Will Rogers, *The Autobiography of Will Rogers* (Boston: Houghton Mifflin, 1949), p. 394.

2. Bryan B. Sterling, *The Will Rogers Scrapbook* (New York: Grosset & Dunlap, 1976), p. 47.

3. Richard M. Ketchum, *Will Rogers: His Life and Times* (New York: American Heritage, 1973), p. 368.

4. Ibid., p. 369.

5. Bryan B. Sterling and Frances N. Sterling, *A Will Rogers Treasury* (New York: Crown, 1982), p. 267.

6. Homer Croy, *Our Will Rogers* (New York: Duell, Sloan and Pearce, 1953), p. 299.

7. Ketchum, p. 390.

8. John O'Connor, "A Man of the People, A Symbol of His Time," *The New York Times*, November 30, 1988, p. C18.

Further Reading

Croy, Homer. *Our Will Rogers*. New York: Duell, Sloan and Pearce, 1953.

Day, Donald. *Will Rogers: A Biography*. New York: McKay, 1962.

Ketchum, Richard M. *Will Rogers: His Life and Times*. New York: American Heritage, 1973.

Richards, Kenneth G. *People of Destiny: Will Rogers*. Chicago: Children's Press, 1968.

Rogers, Betty. *Will Rogers: His Wife's Story*. Indianapolis: Bobbs-Merrill, 1941.

Rogers, Will. *The Autobiography of Will Rogers*. Boston: Houghton Mifflin, 1949.

Sterling, Bryan B. *The Will Rogers Scrapbook*. New York: Grosset and Dunlap, 1976.

Sterling, Bryan B., and Frances N. Sterling. *A Will Rogers Treasury*. New York: Crown Publishers, 1982.

Trent, Spi. *My Cousin Will Rogers*. New York: G. P. Putnam, 1938.

Yagoda, Ben. *Will Rogers: A Biography*. New York: Knopf, 1993.

Index